LANGUAGE!

The Comprehensive Literacy Curriculum

Jane Fell Greene, Ed.D.

SOPRIS WEST EDUCATIONAL SERVICES
A CAMBIUM LEARNING COMPANY

BOSTON, MA • NEW YORK, NY • LONGMONT, CO

12 13 14 15   HPS   13 12 11 10

Editorial Director: Nancy Chapel Eberhardt
Word and Phrase Selection: Judy Fell Woods
English Learners: Jennifer Wells Greene
Lesson Development: Sheryl Ferlito, Donna Lutz
Morphology: John Alexander, Mike Minsky, Bruce Rosow
Text Selection: Sara Buckerfield, Jim Cloonan
Decodable Text: Jenny Hamilton, Steve Harmon

ISBN 13 Digit: 978-1-59318-322-6
ISBN 10 Digit: 1-59318-322-4

Printed in the United States of America

Published and distributed by

Cambium
LEARNING®
Sopris West®

4093 Specialty Place • Longmont, CO 80504 • (303) 651-2829
www.sopriswest.com

70877/10-10

Table of Contents

Check off the activities you complete with each lesson. Evaluate your accomplishments at the end of each lesson. Pay attention to teacher evaluations and comments.

Unit Objectives	Lesson 1 (Date:_____)	Lesson 2 (Date:_____)
STEP 1 **Phonemic Awareness and Phonics** • Say the sounds for the consonant <u>x</u> (/ gz /). • Write the letter for the sounds / g / + / z /. • Say the short vowel sound for the vowel <u>e</u> (/ ĕ /). • Write the letter for the short vowel sound / ĕ /. • Identify syllables in spoken words.	❑ Move It and Mark It ❑ Phonemic Drills ❑ See and Say ❑ Exercise 1: Say and Write ❑ Handwriting Practice (as needed)	❑ Using the Vowel Chart (T) ❑ Diacritical Marks: Signaling Short Vowel Sounds ❑ Phonemic Drills ❑ See and Say
STEP 2 **Word Recognition and Spelling** • Read and spell words with sound-spelling correspondences from this and previous units. • Read and spell the **Essential Words**: *all, call, into, our, small, their.* • Read and spell contractions with **not**.	❑ Exercise 2: Spelling Pretest 1 ❑ Build It, Bank It ❑ Memorize It	❑ Build It, Bank It ❑ Word Fluency 1 ❑ Memorize It ❑ Handwriting Practice
STEP 3 **Vocabulary and Morphology** • Define **Unit Vocabulary** words. • Write plural nouns and third person singular, present tense verbs that take -**es**. • Write the past tense. • Distinguish homophones in context.	❑ Unit Vocabulary ❑ Multiple Meaning Map (T) ❑ Expression of the Day	❑ Exercise 1: Find It: -**es** Endings ❑ Exercise 2: Add It: -**es** Endings ❑ Exercise 3: Rewrite It: Changing Verb Form ❑ Expression of the Day
STEP 4 **Grammar and Usage** • Identify and write regular past tense verbs. • Distinguish present and past tense verbs. • Combine subjects to form a compound subject.	❑ Exercise 3: Identify It: Concrete or Abstract Nouns	❑ Exercise 4: Find It: Subjects ❑ Exercise 5: Sort It: Subjects (T) ❑ Introduction: Possessives ❑ Exercise 6: Find It: Possessive Pronouns
STEP 5 **Listening and Reading Comprehension** • Use context clues to define a new word. • Identify signal words to answer questions. • Select the main idea of each paragraph and identify transition words in classification text.	❑ Exercise 4: Phrase It ❑ Read It: "The World on the Web" ❑ Exercise 5: Find It: Words With / ĕ /	❑ Passage Fluency 1
STEP 6 **Speaking and Writing** • Generate sentences using **Unit Vocabulary**. • Distinguish fact and opinion sentences. • Identify signal words to answer questions. • Identify main ideas and transition words in text.	❑ Masterpiece Sentences: Stages 1–4	❑ Sentence Types: Fact or Opinion?

Self-Evaluation (5 is the highest)
  Effort = I produced my best work.
  Participation = I was actively involved in tasks.
  Independence = I worked on my own.
	Effort: 1 2 3 4 5
	Participation: 1 2 3 4 5
	Independence: 1 2 3 4 5
		Effort: 1 2 3 4 5
		Participation: 1 2 3 4 5
		Independence: 1 2 3 4 5

Teacher Evaluation	**Effort:** 1 2 3 4 5 **Participation:** 1 2 3 4 5 **Independence:** 1 2 3 4 5	**Effort:** 1 2 3 4 5 **Participation:** 1 2 3 4 5 **Independence:** 1 2 3 4 5

Lesson 3 (Date:_____)	**Lesson 4** (Date:_____)	**Lesson 5** (Date:_____)
❑ Phonemic Drills ❑ Exercise 1: Listening for Sounds in Words	❑ Phonemic Drills ❑ Exercise 1: Listening for Sounds in Words ❑ Letter-Sound Fluency	❑ Phonemic Drills ❑ Letter-Sound Fluency ❑ Exercise 1: Say and Write ❑ Content Mastery: Sound-Spelling Correspondences
❑ Exercise 2: Listening for Word Parts ❑ Exercise 3: Add It: Spelling Words With **-es** ❑ Word Fluency 1 ❑ Exercise 4: Find It: Essential Words	❑ Chain It ❑ Double It (T) ❑ Word Fluency 2 ❑ Type It ❑ Handwriting Practice	❑ Content Mastery: Spelling Posttest 1 ❑ Exercise 2: Sort It: Sounds for **-ed** (T)
❑ Exercise 5: Word Networks: Homophones ❑ Draw It: Idioms ❑ Expression of the Day	❑ Exercise 2: Find It: Past Tense ❑ Exercise 3: Sort It: Sounds for **-ed** ❑ Exercise 4: Add It and Identify It ❑ Expression of the Day	❑ Multiple Meaning Map (T) ❑ Expression of the Day
❑ Introduction: Past Tense ❑ Exercise 6: Identify It: Past Tense ❑ Exercise 7: Rewrite It: Past Tense	❑ Verb Tense ❑ Exercise 5: Sort It: Verb Tense	❑ Masterpiece Sentences: Stages 1–6 ❑ Masterpiece Sentences: Changing Past to Present Tense
❑ Instructional Text: "World Wide Web" ❑ Exercise 8: Use the Clues	❑ Exercise 6: Blueprint for Reading: Identifying Main Ideas (T)	❑ Blueprint for Reading Introduction to Transition Words (T)
❑ Exercise 9: Answer It	❑ Blueprint for Writing: Topic and Main Ideas (T) ❑ Challenge Text: "Super Webs"	❑ Blueprint for Writing: Adding Transition Words (T) ❑ Write It: Summary Paragraph ❑ Challenge Text: "Super Webs"
Effort: 1 2 3 4 5 **Participation:** 1 2 3 4 5 **Independence:** 1 2 3 4 5	**Effort:** 1 2 3 4 5 **Participation:** 1 2 3 4 5 **Independence:** 1 2 3 4 5	**Effort:** 1 2 3 4 5 **Participation:** 1 2 3 4 5 **Independence:** 1 2 3 4 5
Effort: 1 2 3 4 5 **Participation:** 1 2 3 4 5 **Independence:** 1 2 3 4 5	**Effort:** 1 2 3 4 5 **Participation:** 1 2 3 4 5 **Independence:** 1 2 3 4 5	**Effort:** 1 2 3 4 5 **Participation:** 1 2 3 4 5 **Independence:** 1 2 3 4 5

Lesson Checklist
Lessons 6–7

Check off the activities you complete with each lesson. Evaluate your accomplishments at the end of each lesson. Pay attention to teacher evaluations and comments.

Unit Objectives	Lesson 6 (Date:_____)	Lesson 7 (Date:_____)
STEP 1 — Phonemic Awareness and Phonics • Say the sounds for the consonant **x** (/ gz /). • Write the letter for the sounds / g / + / z /. • Say the short vowel sound for the vowel **e** (/ ĕ /). • Write the letter for the short vowel sound / ĕ /. • Identify syllables in spoken words.	❑ Phonemic Drills ❑ Move It and Mark It ❑ See and Say ❑ Handwriting Practice ❑ Syllable Awareness: Segmentation	❑ Phonemic Drills ❑ See and Name ❑ Name and Write ❑ Syllable Awareness: Deletion
STEP 2 — Word Recognition and Spelling • Read and spell words with sound-spelling combinations from this and previous units. • Read and spell the **Essential Words**: all, call, into, small, our, their. • Read and spell contractions with **not**.	❑ Exercise 1: Spelling Pretest 2 ❑ Build It, Bank It ❑ Word Fluency 3	❑ Introduction: Contractions ❑ Exercise 1: Contract It ❑ Double It (T)
STEP 3 — Vocabulary and Morphology • Define **Unit Vocabulary** words. • Write plural nouns and third person singular, present tense verbs that take **-es**. • Write the past tense. • Distinguish homophones in context.	❑ Unit Vocabulary ❑ Exercise 2: Sort It: Meaning Categories (T) ❑ Expression of the Day	❑ Exercise 2: Rewrite It: Past Tense ❑ Exercise 3: More Rewrite It: Past Tense ❑ Expression of the Day
STEP 4 — Grammar and Usage • Identify and write regular past tense verbs. • Distinguish present and past tense. • Combine subjects to form a compound subject.	❑ Exercise 3: Combine It: Compound Subjects	❑ Exercise 4: Expand It: Compound Subjects
STEP 5 — Listening and Reading Comprehension • Use context clues to define a new word. • Identify signal words to answer questions. • Select the main idea of each paragraph and identify transition words in classification text.	❑ Exercise 4: Phrase It ❑ Read It: "Log On!" ❑ Exercise 5: Find It: Words With / ĕ /	❑ Passage Fluency 2
STEP 6 — Speaking and Writing • Generate sentences using **Unit Vocabulary**. • Distinguish fact and opinion sentences. • Identify signal words to answer questions. • Identify main ideas and transition words in text.	❑ Masterpiece Sentences: Stage 1 ❑ Using Masterpiece Sentences	❑ Information: Fact or Opinion?
Self-Evaluation (5 is the highest) **Effort** = I produced my best work. **Participation** = I was actively involved in tasks. **Independence** = I worked on my own.	**Effort:** 1 2 3 4 5 **Participation:** 1 2 3 4 5 **Independence:** 1 2 3 4 5	**Effort:** 1 2 3 4 5 **Participation:** 1 2 3 4 5 **Independence:** 1 2 3 4 5
Teacher Evaluation	**Effort:** 1 2 3 4 5 **Participation:** 1 2 3 4 5 **Independence:** 1 2 3 4 5	**Effort:** 1 2 3 4 5 **Participation:** 1 2 3 4 5 **Independence:** 1 2 3 4 5

Lesson 8 (Date:_____)	Lesson 9 (Date:_____)	Lesson 10 (Date:_____)
❏ Phonemic Drills ❏ Letter-Name Fluency ❏ Exercise 1: Syllable Awareness: Segmentation	❏ Phonemic Drills ❏ Letter-Name Fluency ❏ Exercise 1: Syllable Awareness: Segmentation	❏ Exercise 1: Listening for Sounds in Words
❏ Exercise 2: Listening for Word Parts ❏ Exercise 3: Sort It: Short Vowels ❏ Word Fluency 4	❏ Exercise 2: Sentence Dictation ❏ Double It (T)	❏ Content Mastery: Spelling Posttest 2
❏ Exercise 4: Word Networks: Synonyms ❏ Content Mastery: Word Relationships	❏ Exercise 3: Identify It: Nouns or Verbs ❏ Exercise 4: Find It: Noun and Verb Forms ❏ Expression of the Day	❏ Define It (T) ❏ Draw It: Idioms ❏ Expression of the Day
❏ Exercise 5: Diagram It: Subject + Subject / Predicate (T)	❏ Masterpiece Sentences: Stages 1–6 ❏ Using Masterpiece Sentences: Compound Subjects	❏ Content Mastery: Past Tense ❏ Content Mastery: Compound Subjects
❏ Instructional Text: "Web of Lies" ❏ Exercise 6: Use the Clues	❏ Instructional Text: "Web Wins!"	❏ Exercise 2: Take Note: Information (T)
❏ Exercise 7: Answer It	❏ Exercise 5: Answer It ❏ Challenge Text: "The Spider's Thread"	❏ Exercise 2: Take Note: Information (T) ❏ Summary Writing: Current Event ❏ Challenge Text: "Spider Woman"
Effort: 1 2 3 4 5 **Participation:** 1 2 3 4 5 **Independence:** 1 2 3 4 5	**Effort:** 1 2 3 4 5 **Participation:** 1 2 3 4 5 **Independence:** 1 2 3 4 5	**Effort:** 1 2 3 4 5 **Participation:** 1 2 3 4 5 **Independence:** 1 2 3 4 5
Effort: 1 2 3 4 5 **Participation:** 1 2 3 4 5 **Independence:** 1 2 3 4 5	**Effort:** 1 2 3 4 5 **Participation:** 1 2 3 4 5 **Independence:** 1 2 3 4 5	**Effort:** 1 2 3 4 5 **Participation:** 1 2 3 4 5 **Independence:** 1 2 3 4 5

Exercise 1 · Say and Write

▸ Repeat each sound your teacher says.

▸ Write the letter or letters for the sound.

1. _____   3. _____   5. _____   7. _____   9. _____

2. _____   4. _____   6. _____   8. _____   10. _____

Exercise 2 · Spelling Pretest 1

▸ Write the words your teacher repeats.

1. _____   6. _____   11. _____

2. _____   7. _____   12. _____

3. _____   8. _____   13. _____

4. _____   9. _____   14. _____

5. _____   10. _____   15. _____

Exercise 3 · Identify It: Concrete or Abstract Nouns

▸ Read each sentence with your teacher.

▸ Circle the noun that is the subject of the sentence.

▸ Decide if the subject noun is a *person*, *place*, or *thing* (concrete) or an *idea* (abstract).

▸ Print C for concrete or A for abstract on the blank line after the sentence.

▸ The first sentence is done for you.

1. (Letters) did not travel fast in the past.   C

   Letters answers "Who (or what) did it?" *Letters* is the subject.

2. Letters had to have stamps. _____

3. The Web did not exist in the past. _____

4. In the past, students wrote reports. _____

5. Facts were hard to get. _____

6. A student spent days getting facts. _____

7. The Internet has many facts that help students. _____

8. An index on the Web can have endless lists. _____

9. The WWW can give you facts in a snap. _____

10. The Web sends facts to your desktop. _____

Unit 7 · Lesson 1

Exercise 4 · Phrase It

▸ Read each sentence.

▸ Use the penciling strategy to "scoop" the phrases in each sentence.

▸ Read them as you would say them.

▸ The first two are done for you to copy below.

 1. Log on.

    Log on.

 2. Kids log on to the World Wide Web.

    Kids log on to the World Wide Web.

 3. They get facts from the Web.

 4. The Web sends facts to their desktops.

 5. Kids use facts to draft their texts.

 6. The Web has facts on all topics.

 7. Look at the past.

 8. The Web did not exist.

 9. It gives us facts in a snap.

 10. The Web spans the world.

Exercise 5 · Find It: Words With / ĕ /

▶ Read this text.

▶ Highlight one-syllable words with / ĕ /.

▶ Write five of the / ĕ / words on the lines below the reading.

---

from the "World Wide Web"

Kids log on to the World Wide Web. It is the Internet. Kids call it the Web. They get text from the Web. Kids scan text. Kids look for facts. They get films on the Web. Kids scan the film clips. The Web sends facts to their desktop. It spans the planet.

Log on. Getting facts is quick. It is a snap. Step on an express track. The Web has facts on all topics. Kids use PCs. PCs help get the facts. Kids use them to draft their text. PCs let kids edit the facts. They print the text. The job ends. Kids do their jobs fast.

---

1. _____

2. _____

3. _____

4. _____

5. _____

Exercise 1 · Find It: -es Endings

▸ Read the sentences.

▸ Underline the verbs with the -es ending.

    1. Lin-Lin misses her pets.

    2. Ted mixes his ham and eggs in the pan.

    3. Fred fixes his mom's laptop.

    4. Lin-Yan faxes Pablo the rest of the text.

    5. Jan presses her silk pants.

▸ Go back and circle the subject in each sentence.

▸ The subjects in the sentences are all: First person   Second person   Third person
  (underline one)   singular   singular   singular

▸ Why can't we just add <u>s</u> to these verbs?

_____

_____

Exercise 2 · Add It: -es Endings

▸ Read each sentence.

▸ Add the **-es** suffix to the verb to make the sentence correct.

▸ Reread the sentence to check your work.

Examples:
Mom kiss __es__ Nell on the neck.
The pop fizz __es__ in the glass.
Lin fix __es__ the desk.

1. Ling-Ling pass _____ the jam.

2. Max mix _____ the eggs.

3. Inez wax _____ the van.

4. Linda dress _____ the mascot.

5. Gamal fax _____ the text.

6. The dog miss _____ Ted.

7. The cab pass _____ on the left.

8. The dog mess _____ with the cat.

9. Ken press _____ his pants.

10. Kim box _____ the mints.

Unit 7 · Lesson 2

Exercise 3 · Rewrite It: Changing Verb Form

▸ Read the present progressive verb form sentence.

▸ Underline the present progressive verb phrase.

▸ Rewrite the verb in the third person singular present tense.

▸ Read the new sentence.

Present Progressive Form (is rocking)	Third person singular present tense (mixes, messes, fizzes)
Examples:	**Examples:**
Greg's van is passing the red cab.	Greg's van _**passes**_ the red cab.
Irma is fixing the gasket for Max.	Irma _**fixes**_ the gasket for Max.
1. Max is mixing eggs for a snack.	**1.** Max _____ eggs for a snack.
2. Irma is faxing Scott the test.	**2.** Irma _____ Scott the test.
3. Lin-Yan is tossing her cap in the backpack.	**3.** Lin-Yan _____ her cap in the backpack.
4. Jack is waxing the van.	**4.** Jack _____ the van.
5. Hon is fixing the film for the band.	**5.** Hon _____ the film for the band.
6. Lim is missing Jack's visit.	**6.** Lim _____ Jack's visit.
7. Ted is crossing the pond on a raft.	**7.** Ted _____ the pond on a raft.
8. Pancho is missing the trip.	**8.** Pancho _____ the trip.
9. Jeff is stressing out about the lost dog.	**9.** Jeff _____ out about the lost dog.
10. Nell is expressing herself well to Ken.	**10.** Nell _____ herself well to Ken.

Exercise 4 · Find It: Subjects

▸ Read each sentence and find the subject.

▸ Underline the subject noun or pronoun in each sentence.

▸ The first sentence is done for you.

1. <u>IM</u> lets kids get online fast and spend (their) time visiting.

2. Some kids can't exist if they aren't on IM.

3. They can all send their IMs back fast.

4. The text in IM isn't long and isn't exact.

5. Your spelling isn't edited.

6. Messages are fast, but aren't exact.

7. Ben didn't think that he should do IM in his math class.

8. I said to Ben, "Can't you exit when the bell rings for class?"

9. In our class, there were six kids who didn't stop IM when the bell rang.

10. Mr. West inspected all of our PCs and kept our class in until he had finished.

11. The best spot to do IM is not in our math class!

Exercise 5 · Sort It: Subjects

▸ Listen to each sentence in Exercise 4, **Find It**, and review the underlined subject nouns.

▸ Decide if the underlined nouns are people, places, or things.

▸ Write the underlined subject nouns in the correct column in the chart below.

People	Places	Things

Exercise 6 · Find It: Possessives

▸ Reread the sentences in Exercise 4, **Find It: Subjects**.

▸ Circle the possessive adjectives.

▸ Write the possessive adjectives you find on the lines.

_____

_____

_____

_____

Lesson 3

Exercise 1 · Listening for Sounds in Words

▸ Listen to each word your teacher says.

▸ Put an X where you hear the / *gz* / sound.

▸ If you do not hear / *gz* /, write the letters for the sounds in the word in the boxes.

1.

2.

3.

4.

5.

(continued)

▶ Put an X where you hear the / *ks* / sound.

▶ If you do not hear / *ks* /, write the letters for the sounds in the word in the boxes.

6. ☐☐☐

7. ☐☐☐

8. ☐☐☐☐

9. ☐☐☐☐

10. ☐☐☐☐☐

Exercise 2 · Listening for Word Parts

▸ Listen to each word.

▸ Write the word part your teacher repeats.

1. _____   6. _____

2. _____   7. _____

3. _____   8. _____

4. _____   9. _____

5. _____   10. _____

Exercise 3 · Add It: Spelling Words With -es

1. Read the words in each column.

▸ Look for the pattern in the words in each column. What is it?

▸ Write the pattern name in the space at the top of each column.

Pattern: _____ _____	Pattern: _____ _____	Pattern: _____ _____
bless _____	frizz _____	flex _____
class _____	fizz _____	ax _____
hiss _____		fox _____
		mix _____

2. Add **-es** to each word above. Write the word in the blank next to the word.

3. When do we use **-es**?

_____

_____

_____

Unit 7 · Lesson 3

Exercise 4 · Find It: Essential Words

▸ Find the Unit 7 **Essential Words** in these sentences.

▸ Underline the words. There may be more than one in a sentence.

▸ Circle the three **Essential Words** that rhyme.

1. All of the men got on the Web.

2. Did the vet call you?

3. We sent our rabbit to the vet.

4. Spiders spin small silk webs.

5. Spiders tempt insects into their webs.

▸ Write the **Essential Words** in the spaces.

_____   _____   _____

_____   _____   _____

Exercise 5 · Word Networks: Homophones

▸ Write the words **their** and **there** on the lines in the Venn diagram.

▸ Fill in information about both words.

▸ Identify what is the same about the two words.

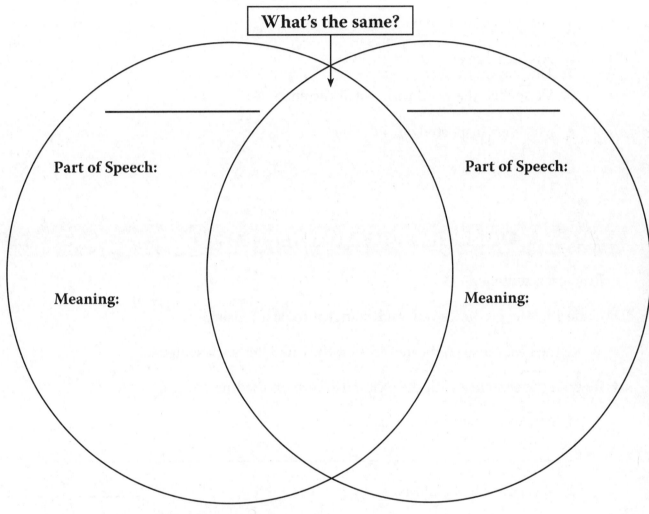

What's the same?

Part of Speech:

Meaning:

Part of Speech:

Meaning:

▸ Fill in the blanks with **their** or **there**.

1. The spider's web is over _____ .

2. _____ webs are made of silk.

3. How did the web get _____ ?

4. _____ dragline silk is stronger than steel wire.

5. The spider web is _____ in a dark corner.

Unit 7 · Lesson 3

Exercise 6 · Identify It: Past Tense

▸ Read each sentence and find the verbs with **-ed** endings.

▸ Underline the verbs with **-ed** endings.

▸ The first sentence is done for you.

1. Ben <u>edited</u> his e-mail.

2. His message existed on his PC.

3. He spelled the word with **-ed** at the end.

4. Mr. West inspected our PCs.

5. He stopped the test.

Exercise 7 · Rewrite It: Past Tense

▸ Read each sentence.

▸ Underline the predicate verb and change it to past tense form.

▸ Write the past tense predicate verbs on the line after each sentence.

▸ Rewrite the sentence with the past tense verb on the line.

1. Mr. West inspects our class. _____

_____

2. Ben edits all of his IMs. _____

_____

3. He helps me with spelling. _____

_____

4. Mr. West checks every problem on our math tests. _____

_____

5. Mr. West said that he invests in kids. _____

_____

Exercise 8 · Use the Clues

▸ Use context clues to define **immediate**.

▸ Underline the vocabulary word.

▸ Read the text surrounding the unknown word.

▸ Identify and underline the words that help define the unknown word.

▸ Draw arrows to show the link between the underlined words and the unknown word.

---

from "World Wide Web"

First, we know that we can find information on the Web fast. Do you use the Web for reports? Think about this. Before the Internet, where would you get information? You would have used many books. You would have spent dozens of hours searching. That would not happen today! Today, if you need information, it's on the Web. It's at your fingertips. We can even get photographs. We can download them. Some come from the moon! We see them just as they're sent to Earth. That's not just fast. It's immediate.

Define It

immediate: _____

▸ Verify your definition with a dictionary or www.yourdictionary.com.

Unit 7 · Lesson 3

Exercise 9 · Answer It

▸ Drop the signal word in each question.

▸ Begin your answer with the remainder of the question.

▸ Check for sentence signals—capital letters and end punctuation.

1. **State** the meaning of WWW.

   _____

2. **Name** the process used to get photographs from the Internet.

   _____

   _____

3. How do you **recognize** the differences among the endings on Web addresses?

   _____

   _____

   _____

   _____

4. **Locate** the items that can be found on a home page.

   _____

   _____

5. **How** has e-mail changed communication?

   _____

   _____

   _____

Exercise 1 · Listening for Sounds in Words

▶ Listen to each word your teacher says.

▶ Repeat each word.

▶ Put an X in the column to show the last sound or sounds you hear.

	/ t /	/ d /	/ ĭd /
1.			
2.			
3.			
4.			
5.			
6.			
7.			
8.			
9.			
10.			

Unit 7 · Lesson 4

Exercise 2 · Find It: Past Tense

▸ Listen as your teacher reads the sentences.

▸ Underline the verbs.

▸ Pay attention to the verb endings.

1. Bob grabbed a laptop to get on the web.

2. Lin-Lin pegged a tag on her computer.

3. Fidel's father passed the cab.

4. Fidel fixed the desktop.

5. Rosa intended to get the best computer.

6. Ted rested at the clinic.

7. The man passed the fan to Stan.

8. Ethel helped her husband Jed.

9. The crash dented Lisa's van.

10. Jack jazzed up his act.

Exercise 3 · Sort It: Sounds for -ed

▸ Sort the **-ed** verbs from the sentences in Exercise 2, **Find It**, into the groups below by the way **-ed** is pronounced.

/ t / (messed)	/ d / (mobbed)	/ ĭd / (mended)

▸ Write the base verbs (without the **-ed**) from the / ĭd / column above.

_____

▸ When is the suffix **-ed** pronounced / ĭd / and not / t / or / d / ?

_____

Unit 7 · Lesson 4

Exercise 4 · Add It and Identify It

▸ Add the past tense suffix to each word in the first column.

▸ Write the word with the new ending in the second column.

▸ Read the past tense verb.

▸ X the sound that **-ed** makes in the past tense verb.

Add the suffix (mobbed, messed, mended)	Write the word	-ed sound		
		/ t /	/ d /	/ ĭd /
Examples: help_ed_	_____helped_____	x		
smell_ed_	_____smelled_____		x	
rent_ed_	_____rented_____			x
1. melt_____	_____			
2. press_____	_____			
3. block_____	_____			
4. fill_____	_____			
5. pass_____	_____			
6. crack_____	_____			
7. spill_____	_____			
8. frisk_____	_____			
9. fax_____	_____			
10. stack_____	_____			

Exercise 5 · Sort It: Verb Tense

▸ Read each pair of sentences.

▸ Sort the 20 underlined verbs into the three categories in the chart below.

1. They <u>ended</u> their project.   They had to <u>end</u> their project.

2. In spring, the robin <u>nests</u>.   The robins <u>nested</u> in spring.

3. He <u>rests</u> after PE class.   He <u>rested</u> after PE class.

4. It had all <u>melted</u>.   When will it all <u>melt</u>?

5. She <u>called</u> them into their class.   She <u>calls</u> them into their class.

6. Can you <u>edit</u> this for him?   You <u>edited</u> this for him.

7. Gossip and chitchat don't <u>help</u>.   She <u>helped</u> stop gossip and chitchat.

8. The Internet <u>gets</u> you there fast!   The Internet can <u>get</u> you there fast.

9. They <u>smelled</u> a rat.   Did they <u>smell</u> a rat?

10. Mr. West <u>asks</u> the class to finish fast.   Mr. West <u>asked</u> the class to finish fast.

Base verb	Present Tense, Third Person Singular verb form (-s or -es ending)	Past Tense verb form (-ed ending)

Unit 7 · Lesson 4

Exercise 6 · Blueprint for Reading: Identifying Main Ideas

▶ Highlight the main idea of each paragraph in blue.

---

from "World Wide Web"

First, we know that we can find information on the Web fast. Do you use the Web for reports? Think about this. Before the Internet, where would you get information? You would have used many books. You would have spent dozens of hours searching. That would not happen today. Today, if you need information, it's on the Web. It's at your fingertips. We can even get photographs. We can download them. Some come from the moon! We see them just as they're sent to Earth. That's not just fast. It's immediate!

Second, the Web has its own address system. The Web has millions of links. Finding one Web site could become a cyberspace nightmare! But the Web solves that problem. At home, your address might be 1111 Main Street. On the Web, you can have an address. Your Web address could be: **roberto.en.utexas.edu**. Who is Roberto? That's the person at the web address. The **.en** means English Department. The end, **.edu**, stands for education. There are other endings. The ending **.com** means commercial. The ending **.gov** means government. The ending **.au** means Australia. What about the address that begins with **utexas**? That one is unique. It stands for University of Texas. Look at your school's Web address. Can you explain how its address identifies the school?

Also, the Web is organized in a special way. It is made up of home pages. Home pages are usually the first pages you see on a Web site. The pages contain lots

(continued)

of things. They may be just words. They may have pictures. Most home pages have both. Many have video. A page might tell about a company. It might tell about a school. It could tell about a person or a subject. How do we interact with a home page? We choose a link. We click on it. We get information! Most home pages link to many other pages.

Finally, the Web has e-mail. E-mail has changed communication. Today, we connect in a new way. We can talk to anybody, any place, any time. In seconds, we contact someone. They can be across the planet. It doesn't matter. E-mail saves us time. It helps us work quickly. We can even keep records of our work in special mailboxes. But e-mail is fun, too. It keeps us in touch with friends. Do you think e-mail has affected postal mail? Do you think it has affected telephone calls? How do you see the future of Web communication?

Lesson 5

Exercise 1 · Say and Write

▸ Repeat each sound your teacher says.

▸ Write the letter or letters for the sound.

▸ Add the correct diacritical mark (breve) over the vowel letter to signal the short vowel sound.

1. _____   2. _____   3. _____   4. _____   5. _____

6. _____   7. _____   8. _____   9. _____   10. _____

Exercise 2 · Sort It: Sounds for -ed

▸ Sort the words in the box according to the sounds for **-ed**: / t /, / d /, / ĭd /.

called	begged	belted	stressed	tested	petted
yelled	helped	rented	quacked	faxed	webbed

▸ Write the words under the correct sound for **-ed**.

/ t /	/ d /	/ ĭd /

Exercise 1 · Spelling Pretest

▸ Write the words your teacher repeats.

1. _____	6. _____	11. _____
2. _____	7. _____	12. _____
3. _____	8. _____	13. _____
4. _____	9. _____	14. _____
5. _____	10. _____	15. _____

Unit 7 · Lesson 6

Exercise 2 · Sort It: Meaning Categories

▸ Read the words in the box.

Web	desk	desktop
asset	invest	fax
credit	net	disk
lend	sell	

▸ Sort the words into the two template categories based on meaning.

▸ Write the words in the template columns.

Hint: One word can be used in both columns. In one column, the first letter should be capitalized.

Computers	Money

Exercise 3 · Combine It: Compound Subjects

▸ Read the following pairs of sentences.

▸ Combine the subjects into a new sentence, using the conjunction **and**.

▸ Write the new sentence on the line below the sentence pairs.

▸ Circle the compound subject elements.

▸ The first sentence is done for you.

1. Ben got help.   Kim got help.

(Ben) and (Kim) got help.

2. The egg was fresh.   The milk was fresh.

_____

3. The dress was hemmed.   The pants were hemmed.

_____

4. Min sat on the steps.   I sat on the steps.

_____

5. An elk ran on this strip.   A rabbit ran on this strip.

_____

6. You will pass the test.   I will pass the test.

_____

7. My class had a profit.   Your class had a profit.

_____

(continued)

Exercise 3 *(continued)* · Combine It: Compound Subjects

8. The desk was polished.   The lamp was polished.

_____

9. Ants are insects.   Bees are insects.

_____

10. Frank had a credit at the bank.   I had a credit at the bank.

_____

Exercise 4 · Phrase It

▸ Read each sentence.

▸ Use the penciling strategy to "scoop" the phrases in each sentence.

▸ Read as you would speak them.

▸ The first two are done for you to copy below.

1. In the past, mail was not fast.

   In the past, mail was not fast.

2. The Web lets you skip steps.

   The Web lets you skip steps.

3. Sending mail can be quick.

4. A computer lets you draft text.

5. Lots of kids log on.

6. Text is sent to pals.

7. Kids chat online.

8. Kids spend lots of time on the Web.

9. In the past, the TV was on a lot.

10. TV lost the top spot.

Exercise 5 · Find It: Words With / ĕ /

▸ Highlight one-syllable words with / ĕ /.

---

from "Log On!"

Kids spend lots of time on the Web. In the past, the TV was on a lot. Now, it's on less. Kids are logged on. This is a new trend. How can we tell? A survey was drafted. It asked how kids spend their time. What topped the list? Kids picked the Web. TV lost the top spot.

Adults have a job. Ads are sent on the Web. Ads can tempt kids. Kids can be misled. They can be tricked. Adults have to inspect the ads. They can block the bad ads. They look at what is sent. They scan what their kids send back. They inspect the sites kids visit. Adults can have a big impact.

▸ Write five different / ĕ / words on the lines below.

1. _____

2. _____

3. _____

4. _____

5. _____

Lesson 7

Exercise 1 · Contract It

▸ Read each contraction.

▸ Draw a line to the two words that make the contraction.

1. aren't		does not
2. can't		are not
3. didn't		cannot
4. doesn't		did not
5. don't		do not
6. isn't		were not
7. wasn't		is not
8. weren't		was not

(continued)

Unit 7 · Lesson 7

Exercise 1 (continued) · Contract It

▶ Read each contraction in the first column.

▶ Cross out the letter that is "squeezed out" or contracted in the second column.

▶ Write the contraction in the third column.

▶ Read the contraction again.

Read it	Cross out and replace	Rewrite it
1. aren't	aren'ot	
2. can't	cann'ot	
3. didn't	didn'ot	
4. doesn't	doesn'ot	
5. don't	don'ot	
6. isn't	isn'ot	
7. wasn't	wasn'ot	
8. weren't	weren'ot	

Exercise 2 · Rewrite It: Past Tense

▸ Read the verb in the first column.

▸ Cross out any suffixes.

▸ Write the past tense form in the second column.

▸ Read the verb to check your work.

Verb	Past Tense (mobbed, messed, mended)
Examples:	Examples:
stop	stopped
deck	decked
test	tested
webs	webbed
matches	matched
1. jog	
2. bats	
3. quack	
4. web	
5. blesses	
6. net	
7. pens	
8. rent	
9. step	
10. buzzes	

(continued)

Unit 7 · Lesson 7

Exercise 2 (continued) · Rewrite It: Past Tense

▶ Write three complete sentences using any of the past tense verbs.

_____

_____

_____

Exercise 3 · More Rewrite It: Past Tense

▶ Read the present tense sentence in the first column.

▶ Change the verb to the past tense and write it on the blank line in the second column. Remember to double the final consonant when needed.

▶ Read the new sentence.

Present Tense	Past Tense
Examples: Hassan skips bad films. His pals intend to see *Caught in a Web of Lies*.	Hassan __skipped__ bad films. His pals __intended__ to see *Caught in a Web of Lies*.
1. People predict the movie would be a hit.	**1.** People _____ the movie would be a hit.
2. Jenny Li lacks skill in the film.	**2.** Jenny Li _____ skill in the film.
3. She plods through the film with a stiff grin.	**3.** She _____ through the film with a stiff grin.
4. The plot progresses like a long trek on a sick yak.	**4.** The plot _____ like a long trek on a sick yak.
5. They call the film *Caught in a Web of Lies*.	**5.** They _____ the film *Caught in a Web of Lies*.

Exercise 4 · Expand It: Compound Subjects

▸ Listen to the sentences your teacher says.

▸ Write each sentence on the first line.

▸ Underline the subject of each sentence.

▸ For each sentence, add a compound subject and rewrite it on the second line.

▸ Underline the compound subject, including the conjunction **and**.

1. _____

   _____

2. _____

   _____

3. _____

   _____

4. _____

   _____

5. _____

   _____

(continued)

Exercise 4 (continued) · **Expand It: Compound Subjects**

6. _____

_____

7. _____

_____

8. _____

_____

9. _____

_____

10. _____

_____

Exercise 1 · Syllable Awareness: Segmentation

▸ Listen to the word your teacher says.

▸ Repeat the word.

▸ Write the number of syllables in the word.

▸ Write the letter for each vowel sound you hear.

▸ Add the correct diacritical mark (breve) over the word.

	How many syllables do you hear?	First vowel sound	Second vowel sound
1.			
2.			
3.			
4.			
5.			
6.			
7.			
8.			
9.			
10.			

Exercise 2 · Listening for Word Parts

▸ Listen to each word.

▸ Write the word part your teacher repeats.

1. _____   2. _____   3. _____   4. _____   5. _____

6. _____   7. _____   8. _____   9. _____   10. _____

Unit 7 · Lesson 8

Exercise 3 · Sort It: Short Vowels

▸ Sort the word parts from Exercise 2, **Listening for Word Parts**, according to their short vowel sound.

▸ Write the word parts under the correct sound.

/ ĕ /	/ ĭ /	/ ŏ /

Exercise 4 · Word Networks: Synonyms

▸ Write a synonym (same meaning) for the word your teacher says.

▸ Refer to the **Unit Vocabulary** on page 5 of the *Student Text* for your answers.

1. assist _____

2. go _____

3. stop _____

4. transmit _____

5. scent _____

6. obtain _____

7. earn _____

8. exam _____

9. certainly _____

10. fine _____

Exercise 5 · Diagram It: Subject + Subject/Predicate

▸ Review these areas of the diagram with your teacher:

1. Subject: Who (or what) did it?

2. Predicate: What did they (he, she, or it) do?

3. Direct Object: What (or whom) did they do it to?

4. Subject Describers: Which, what kind of, or how many?

5. Predicate Describers: How, when, or where did they do it ?

▸ Read the following sentences with your teacher.

▸ Note the compound subjects, which are underlined.

▸ Diagram each sentence.

▸ The first diagram is done as an example.

1. <u>Chico and I</u> got a fish.

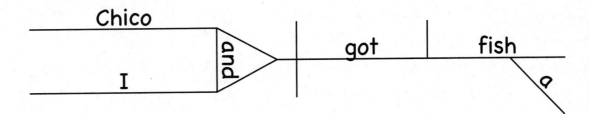

2. The <u>men and their helpers</u> rested.

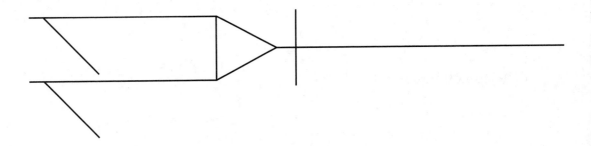

(continued)

Exercise 5 *(continued)* · **Diagram It: Subject + Subject/Predicate**

3. <u>Tessa and her sister</u> collected insects.

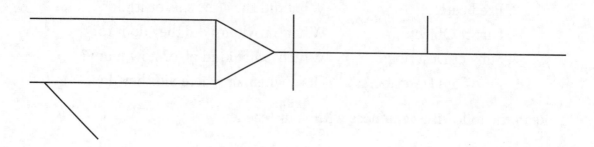

4. Their <u>tent and raft</u> passed the test.

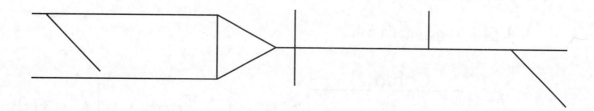

5. <u>Beth and Kim</u> rented a van.

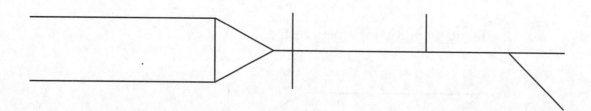

6. <u>Sara and Julio</u> smelled gas.

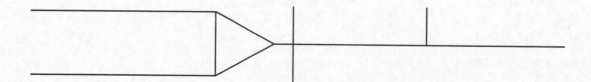

(continued)

7. The <u>vet and I</u> inspected the pets.

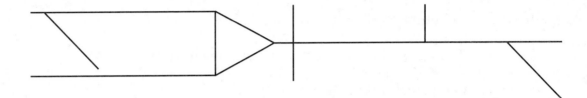

8. The <u>egg and dish</u> cracked.

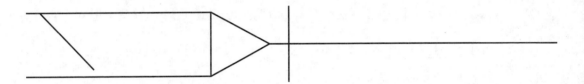

9. <u>Carlo and his dad</u> had jet lag.

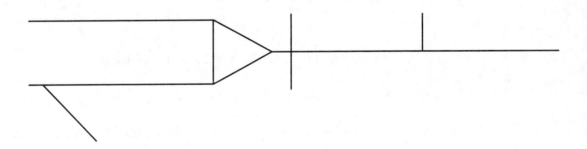

10. <u>Ken and Diego</u> helped the vet.

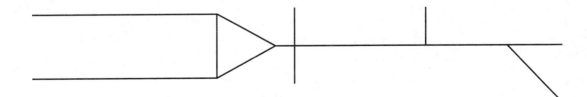

Exercise 6 · Use the Clues

▸ Use word substitutions to define the word **film**.

• Underline the vocabulary word.

• Read text surrounding the unknown word.

• Underline the words that help define the unknown word.

• Circle pronouns that follow the unknown word.

• Draw an arrow to link the surrounding words and pronouns to the unknown word.

> *Caught in a Web of Lies.* It was this summer's hottest movie! You've all heard about it. It had six of Hollywood's hottest stars. One of them was Jenny Li. It had a multi-million dollar budget. *Web of Lies* was predicted to become a top moneymaker. It was going to be a film classic. Last night, I went to see it.

▸ Discuss the other uses of the pronoun **it** to give examples of **film**.

▸ Write a definition of **film** based on the context clues.

▸ Verify your definition with the dictionary or www.yourdictionary.com.

Define It

film: _____

Exercise 7 · Answer It

▸ Answer each question in a complete sentence.

▸ Check for sentence signals—capital letters and end punctuation.

1. List two types of articles found in newspapers.

_____

_____

2. Name the author of the movie review of *Caught in a Web of Lies*.

_____

_____

3. Where did Emilio García work?

_____

_____

4. Choose whether **"Web of Lies"** is a factual article or an opinion article. Explain your answer.

_____

_____

Lesson 9

Exercise 1 · Syllable Awareness: Segmentation

▸ Listen to each word your teacher says.

▸ Repeat the word.

▸ Write the number of syllables in the word.

▸ Write the letter for each vowel sound you hear.

▸ Add the correct diacritical mark (breve) over the vowel letters to signal the short vowel sounds.

	How many syllables do you hear?	First Vowel Sound	Second Vowel Sound	Third Vowel Sound
1.				
2.				
3.				
4.				
5.				
6.				
7.				
8.				
9.				
10.				

Exercise 2 · Sentence Dictation

▶ Listen to each sentence your teacher says.

▶ Repeat the sentence.

▶ Write it on the line.

1. _____

2. _____

3. _____

4. _____

5. _____

▶ Read sentences 1, 2, 4, and 5.

▶ Find the words that follow the **1-1-1** rule.

▶ Write the words on the line.

_____

▶ Rewrite sentences 3 and 5. Replace each contraction with the expanded form.

_____

_____

Unit 7 · Lesson 9

Exercise 3 · Identify It: Nouns or Verbs

▸ Read each sentence.

▸ Look at the underlined word or words in each sentence.

▸ Place an X in the appropriate column to indicate what the underlined word or words are.

Sentences	Nouns		Verbs		
	Plural	Singular possessive	Present Progressive form	Present tense	Past tense
Examples: Lin <u>gets</u> a job at the movie set.				X	
She <u>is hemming</u> a red dress.			X		
It is <u>Jenny Li's</u> best red dress.		X			
Lin <u>expected</u> to meet Jenny.					X
She has seen all of Jenny Li's <u>films</u>.	X				
1. Jenny Li <u>is inspecting</u> her red dress.					
2. She <u>planned</u> to put it on for the new movie, *Caught in a Web of Lies.*					
3. The soda <u>fizzes</u> in her glass.					
4. She just <u>ended</u> a trip to Boston.					
5. <u>Jenny's</u> movie script is on her desk.					
6. Jenny <u>expected</u> to become a big star.					
7. She <u>is acting</u> with the cast.					
8. She <u>bossed</u> the people who work on the set.					
9. She <u>is acting</u> as she always did.					
10. <u>America's</u> sweetheart wins again.					

Exercise 4 · Find It: Noun and Verb Forms

▸ In the first column, read what you need to find.

▸ In the second column, underline the word or words you are asked to find in the sentence.

Can you find…?	Sentence
Examples: Past tense verb	They <u>planned</u> it to be the summer's hottest movie.
Plural noun	For <u>months</u>, we've heard about nothing but *Caught in a Web of Lies*.
1. Third person singular present tense verb	The film opens with Jenny Li, America's sweetheart, in tears (again).
2. Present progressive verb	Jenny (yes, her character's name is also Jenny) is leaving her friends to fly to the Big Apple.
3. Third person singular present tense verb	A friend tells a fib about Jenny.
4. Third person singular present tense verb	Jenny almost misses the plane because she is on her cell phone.
5. Past tense verb	Friends made a web of lies about Jenny.
6. Present progressive verb	Really, she is planning to meet a friend.
7. Present tense verb	That person expects her to be on the plane.
8. Past tense verb	Jenny's friend talked on the phone again.
9. Past tense verb	I napped during this drab movie.
10. Present tense verb	Everyone guesses the ending.

Unit 7 · Lesson 9

Exercise 5 · Answer It

▸ Answer each question in a complete sentence.

▸ Check for sentence signals—capital letters and end punctuation.

1. What was the article about?

   _____

   _____

2. What happened?

   _____

   _____

3. Who polled the teenagers?

   _____

   _____

4. When did the poll take place?

   _____

   _____

5. Where did the teenagers report their answers for the poll?

   _____

   _____

6. What was the result of the poll?

   _____

   _____

Lesson 10

Exercise 1 · Listening for Sounds in Words

▶ Write the letters for the sounds you hear in each word. Remember to use the proper diacritical mark (breve) over vowels.

▶ For words 1–5, circle the word or words with / s / at the end.

▶ Put a box around the word or words with / ĕ / at the beginning.

▶ Write the letters for the sounds you hear in each word. Remember to use the proper diacritical mark (breve) over vowels.

▶ For words 6–10, circle the word or words that rhyme with **pep**.

▶ Put a box around the word or words that rhyme with **lend**.

1.

2.

3.

4.

5.

6.

7.

8.

9.

10.

Unit 7 · Lesson 10

Exercise 2 · Take Note: Information

Key questions for current events	
Topic (**What was the article or program about?**)	_____ _____
Who or what?	_____
What happened?	_____
When?	_____
Where?	_____
Outcome or impact?	_____ _____ _____
Why important?	_____

Current Event Summary

_____

_____

_____

_____

_____

_____

Check off the activities you complete with each lesson. Evaluate your accomplishments at the end of each lesson. Pay attention to teacher evaluations and comments.

Unit Objectives	Lesson 1 (Date:_____)	Lesson 2 (Date:_____)
STEP 1 **Phonemic Awareness and Phonics** • Say the sounds for the consonant digraphs <u>sh</u>, <u>th</u>, <u>ch</u>, <u>wh</u>, and -<u>ng</u>. • Say the sound for the trigraph -<u>tch</u>. • Write the digraphs <u>sh</u>, <u>th</u>, <u>ch</u>, <u>wh</u>, and -<u>ng</u>. • Write the trigraph -<u>tch</u>. • Identify syllables in spoken words.	❑ Move It and Mark it ❑ Phonemic Drills ❑ See and Say ❑ Exercise 1: Say and Write ❑ Exercise 2: Listening for Sounds in Words	❑ Using the Consonant Chart (T) ❑ Phonemic Drills ❑ See and Say
STEP 2 **Word Recognition and Spelling** • Read and spell words with sound-spelling correspondences from this and previous units. • Read and spell the **Essential Words:** *about, any, many, out, word, write.* • Read and spell compound words.	❑ Exercise 3: Spelling Pretest 1 ❑ Build It, Bank It ❑ Memorize It	❑ Build It, Bank It ❑ Word Fluency 1 ❑ Memorize It ❑ Handwriting Practice
STEP 3 **Vocabulary and Morphology** • Define **Unit Vocabulary** words. • Write more plural nouns and third person singular, present tense verbs that take -**es**. • Identify homophones and antonyms with digraphs and trigraphs.	❑ Unit Vocabulary ❑ Multiple Meaning Map (T) ❑ Expression of the Day	❑ Exercise 1: Identify It: Verb Forms ❑ Exercise 2: Rewrite It: Verb Forms ❑ Expression of the Day
STEP 4 **Grammar and Usage** • Identify and write present progressive and past tense verbs. • Identify and write verbs with irregular past tense forms. • Combine predicates to form a compound predicate.	❑ Review: Action Verbs ❑ Review: Multiple Functions of Words	❑ Exercise 3: Find It: Simple Predicate ❑ Exercise 4: Sort It: Present and Past Tense
STEP 5 **Listening and Reading Comprehension** • Read with inflection, phrasing, and expression. • Identify words with digraphs and trigraphs. • Identify transition words in text. • Define new words using context clues.	❑ Exercise 4: Phrase It ❑ Decodable Text: "Singing Whales" ❑ Exercise 5: Find It: Consonant Digraphs	❑ Exercise 5: Find It: Consonant Digraphs (Lesson 1) ❑ Passage Fluency 1
STEP 6 **Speaking and Writing** • Retrieve information and answer questions using complete sentences. • Create **Masterpiece Sentences.** • Create paragraphs from **Blueprint for Writing.**	❑ Masterpiece Sentences: Stages 1 and 2 ❑ Sentence Types: Fact or Opinion?	❑ Exercise 5: Combine It: Compound Subjects
Self-Evaluation (5 is the highest) **Effort** = I produced my best work. **Participation** = I was actively involved in tasks. **Independence** = I worked on my own.	**Effort:** 1 2 3 4 5 **Participation:** 1 2 3 4 5 **Independence:** 1 2 3 4 5	**Effort:** 1 2 3 4 5 **Participation:** 1 2 3 4 5 **Independence:** 1 2 3 4 5
Teacher Evaluation	**Effort:** 1 2 3 4 5 **Participation:** 1 2 3 4 5 **Independence:** 1 2 3 4 5	**Effort:** 1 2 3 4 5 **Participation:** 1 2 3 4 5 **Independence:** 1 2 3 4 5

Lesson 3 (Date:_____)	Lesson 4 (Date:_____)	Lesson 5 (Date:_____)
❏ Consonants and Vowels ❏ Phonemic Drills ❏ Exercise 1: Listening for Sounds in Words	❏ Phonemic Drills ❏ Exercise 1: Listening for Sounds in Words ❏ Letter-Sound Fluency	❏ Phonemic Drills ❏ Letter-Sound Fluency ❏ Exercise 1: Say and Write ❏ Content Mastery: Sound-Spelling Correspondences
❏ Build It, Bank It ❏ Exercise 2: Add It: Using -es ❏ Word Fluency 1 ❏ Exercise 3: Find It: Essential Words	❏ Double It (T) ❏ Word Fluency 2 ❏ Type It ❏ Handwriting Practice	❏ Content Mastery: Spelling Posttest 1 ❏ Exercise 2: Sort It: Consonant Digraphs
❏ Exercise 4: Word Networks: Homophones ❏ Draw It: Idioms ❏ Expression of the Day	❏ Verb Tenses (T) ❏ Exercise 2: Identify It: Past or Present Progressive ❏ Expression of the Day	❏ Multiple Meaning Map (T) ❏ Expression of the Day
❏ Introduction: Irregular Past Tense Verbs ❏ Exercise 5: Identify It: Irregular Past Tense Verbs	❏ Tense Timeline ❏ Exercise 3: Rewrite It: Irregular Past Tense	❏ Masterpiece Sentences: Stages 1–3 ❏ Using Masterpiece Sentences: Changing Past to Present Tense
❏ Instructional Text: "Whale Song" ❏ Exercise 6: Use the Clues	❏ Exercise 4: Blueprint for Reading: Transition Words and Details (T)	❏ Exercise 4: Blueprint for Reading: Transition Words and Details (Lesson 4) ❏ Challenge Text: "Hmong Song"
❏ Exercise 7: Answer It	❏ Blueprint for Writing: Main Ideas and Transition Words (T) ❏ Challenge Text: "Hmong Song"	❏ Blueprint for Writing (T) ❏ Challenge Text: "Hmong Song"
Effort: 1 2 3 4 5 **Participation:** 1 2 3 4 5 **Independence:** 1 2 3 4 5	**Effort:** 1 2 3 4 5 **Participation:** 1 2 3 4 5 **Independence:** 1 2 3 4 5	**Effort:** 1 2 3 4 5 **Participation:** 1 2 3 4 5 **Independence:** 1 2 3 4 5
Effort: 1 2 3 4 5 **Participation:** 1 2 3 4 5 **Independence:** 1 2 3 4 5	**Effort:** 1 2 3 4 5 **Participation:** 1 2 3 4 5 **Independence:** 1 2 3 4 5	**Effort:** 1 2 3 4 5 **Participation:** 1 2 3 4 5 **Independence:** 1 2 3 4 5

Check off the activities you complete with each lesson. Evaluate your accomplishments at the end of each lesson. Pay attention to teacher evaluations and comments.

Unit Objectives	Lesson 6 (Date:_____)	Lesson 7 (Date:_____)
STEP 1 **Phonemic Awareness and Phonics** • Say the sounds for the consonant digraphs <u>sh</u>, <u>th</u>, <u>ch</u>, <u>wh</u>, and <u>-ng</u>. • Say the sound for the trigraph <u>-tch</u>. • Write the digraphs <u>sh</u>, <u>th</u>, <u>ch</u>, <u>wh</u>, and <u>-ng</u>. • Write the trigraph <u>-tch</u>. • Identify syllables in spoken words	❏ Phonemic Drills ❏ Move It and Mark It ❏ Handwriting Practice ❏ Syllable Awareness: Segmentation	❏ Phonemic Drills ❏ Name and Write ❏ Syllable Awareness: Deletion
STEP 2 **Word Recognition and Spelling** • Read and spell words with sound-spelling correspondences from this and previous units. • Read and spell the **Essential Words:** *about, any, many, out, word, write*. • Read and spell compound words.	❏ Exercise 1: Spelling Pretest 2 ❏ Build It, Bank It ❏ Word Fluency 3	❏ Chain It ❏ Exercise 1: Add It: Using -es
STEP 3 **Vocabulary and Morphology** • Define **Unit Vocabulary** words. • Write more plural nouns and third person singular, present tense verbs that take -es. • Identify homophones and antonyms with digraphs and trigraphs.	❏ More About Compound Words ❏ Unit Vocabulary ❏ Exercise 2: Sort It: Meaning Categories ❏ Expression of the Day	❏ Exercise 2: Identify It: Past Tense ❏ Expression of the Day
STEP 4 **Grammar and Usage** • Identify and write present progressive and past tense verbs. • Identify and write verbs with irregular past tense forms. • Combine predicates to form a compound predicate.	❏ Introduction: Compound Predicates ❏ Combine It: Compound Predicates	❏ Exercise 3: Sentence Dictation ❏ Exercise 4: Find It: Compound Predicates
STEP 5 **Listening and Reading Comprehension** • Read with inflection, phrasing, and expression. • Identify words with digraphs and trigraphs. • Identify transition words in text. • Define new words using context clues.	❏ Exercise 3: Phrase It ❏ Decodable Text: "A Man and His Songs" ❏ Exercise 4: Find It: Consonant Digraphs	❏ Exercise 4: Find It: Consonant Digraphs (Lesson 6) ❏ Passage Fluency 2
STEP 6 **Speaking and Writing** • Retrieve information and answer questions using complete sentences. • Create **Masterpiece Sentences**. • Create paragraphs from **Blueprint for Writing**.	❏ Exercise 5: Combine It: Compound Predicates	❏ Masterpiece Sentences: Stage 1 ❏ Using Masterpiece Sentences: Compound Predicates
Self-Evaluation (5 is the highest) **Effort** = I produced my best work. **Participation** = I was actively involved in tasks. **Independence** = I worked on my own.	**Effort:** 1 2 3 4 5 **Participation:** 1 2 3 4 5 **Independence:** 1 2 3 4 5	**Effort:** 1 2 3 4 5 **Participation:** 1 2 3 4 5 **Independence:** 1 2 3 4 5
Teacher Evaluation	**Effort:** 1 2 3 4 5 **Participation:** 1 2 3 4 5 **Independence:** 1 2 3 4 5	**Effort:** 1 2 3 4 5 **Participation:** 1 2 3 4 5 **Independence:** 1 2 3 4 5

Lesson Checklist
Lessons 8–10

Lesson 8 (Date:_____)	Lesson 9 (Date:_____)	Lesson 10 (Date:_____)
❏ Phonemic Drills ❏ Letter-Name Fluency ❏ Exercise 1: Syllable Awareness: Segmentation	❏ Phonemic Drills ❏ Exercise 1: Listening for Sounds in Words ❏ Letter-Name Fluency ❏ Exercise 2: Syllable Awareness: Segmentation	❏ Exercise 1: Listening for Sounds in Words
❏ Exercise 2: Listening for Word Parts ❏ Exercise 3: Sort It: Consonant Digraphs ❏ Word Fluency 4	❏ Exercise 3: Sentence Dictation	❏ Content Mastery: Spelling Posttest 2
❏ Exercise 4: Word Networks: Antonyms ❏ Content Mastery: Word Relationships	❏ Exercise 4: Choose It and Use It: Verb Phrases ❏ Expression of the Day	❏ Exercise 2: Sort It: Meaning Categories ❏ Draw It: Idioms ❏ Expression of the Day
❏ Exercise 5: Diagram It: Subject + Compound Predicate (T)	❏ Exercise 5: Sentence Dictation ❏ Masterpiece Sentences: Stage 2	❏ Content Mastery: Simple Predicate/ Regular and Irregular Verbs/ Compound Predicates
❏ Instructional Text: "Woody's Song" ❏ Exercise 6: Use the Clues	❏ Information: Fact or Opinion?	❏ Instructional Text: "Woody's Song"
❏ Exercise 7: Answer It	❏ Exercise 6: Take Note (T) ❏ Challenge Text: "The Power of Song"	❏ Exercise 6: Take Note (Lesson 9) (T) ❏ Write It: Summary Paragraph (T) ❏ Challenge Text: "The Power of Song"
Effort: 1 2 3 4 5 Participation: 1 2 3 4 5 Independence: 1 2 3 4 5	Effort: 1 2 3 4 5 Participation: 1 2 3 4 5 Independence: 1 2 3 4 5	Effort: 1 2 3 4 5 Participation: 1 2 3 4 5 Independence: 1 2 3 4 5
Effort: 1 2 3 4 5 Participation: 1 2 3 4 5 Independence: 1 2 3 4 5	Effort: 1 2 3 4 5 Participation: 1 2 3 4 5 Independence: 1 2 3 4 5	Effort: 1 2 3 4 5 Participation: 1 2 3 4 5 Independence: 1 2 3 4 5

Exercise 1 · Say and Write

▸ Repeat the sound your teacher says.

▸ Write the letter or letters for the sound in the spaces below.

▸ Add the correct diacritical mark (breve) over the vowel letter to signal the short vowel sound.

1. _____   2. _____   3. _____   4. _____   5. _____

6. _____   7. _____   8. _____   9. _____   10. _____

Exercise 2 · Listening for Sounds in Words

▸ Write the letters __sh__ where you hear the sound / _sh_ / in the words your teacher says.

▸ If you do not hear / _sh_ /, write the letters for the sounds in the word in the boxes.

1.
2.
3.
4.
5.

Exercise 3 · Spelling Pretest 1

▸ Write the words your teacher repeats.

1. _____   6. _____   11. _____

2. _____   7. _____   12. _____

3. _____   8. _____   13. _____

4. _____   9. _____   14. _____

5. _____   10. _____   15. _____

Unit 8 · Lesson 1

Exercise 4 · Phrase It

▸ Use the penciling strategy to "scoop" the phrases in each sentence.

▸ Read as you would speak them.

▸ The first two are done for you.

1. A ship is moving off the dock.

2. It is tracking whales.

3. Whales can sing many pitches.

4. A whale is the biggest living mammal.

5. It can have a fish on its back.

6. It can have a fin on its back.

7. Fish have gills.

8. Whales have lungs.

9. Whales can live in a gam.

10. When you spot a whale, sing with it.

Exercise 5 · Find It: Consonant Digraphs

▸ Quietly read the selection to yourself.

▸ Highlight or underline the words with consonant digraphs.

> **based on "Singing Whales"**
>
> A ship is moving off the dock. Quick, get on. It is tracking whales. Not to catch them. To catch their songs! Whales sing. It's a fact. Their singing is fantastic! They live in the depths, yet their songs get to the top. They can sing at length. A song can last 10 hours! Whales can sing many pitches. The pitch in the song can be shrill. The pitch can be soft. It can blast. Whales can trill in a song. In context, the pitches are a song.

▸ Record five words with five different consonant digraphs on the lines below.

1. _____
2. _____
3. _____
4. _____
5. _____

Exercise 1 · Identify It: Verb Forms

▸ Read each sentence.

▸ Underline the verb or verb phrase.

▸ Decide if the verb is:

- Past tense or

- Present progressive

▸ Mark your choice by putting an X in the correct column.

▸ How did you know? Write the ending that signals time.

(continued)

Exercise 1 (continued) · Identify It: Verb Forms

Sentence	Past Tense (mobbed, messed, mended)	Present Progressive (I am rocking, she is rocking, they are rocking)	How did you know?
Examples: We <u>thanked</u> them for the batch of catfish.	X		–ed
The chimps <u>are flinging</u> sticks.		X	–ing
The chimp <u>is swinging</u> in the branches.		X	–ing
1. The stench of rotten shellfish filled the shop.			
2. The cat snatched all ten shrimp out of the sink.			
3. The fishpond is shrinking in the hot sun.			
4. Beth and Lin are digging a trench for the trash.			
5. The piglets chomped on eggshells and hotdogs.			
6. Chad sketched the ship from his shack.			
7. Lin-Lin is scratching the pink rash on her leg.			
8. Jin is pitching fastballs in the contest.			
9. The rank whiff of catfish shocked Hank.			
10. Jim munched on the shrimp and chips.			

Unit 8 · Lesson 2

Exercise 2 · Rewrite It: Verb Forms

▸ Read the sentences in the first column, which indicate present time.

▸ Circle or highlight the base verb without its ending in the sentence.

▸ Write the base verb in the second column.

▸ Change the base verb to the new verb form as indicated in the third column.

▸ Decide if you need to double the last consonant before adding **-ed** or **-ing**. Write "yes" or "no" in the fourth column.

▸ Write the new verb in the blank in the last column.

▸ Read the new sentence.

Sentence (present tense)	Write the base verb	New verb form	Double the last consonant?	New sentence
Examples: Al mops the eggshells from the deck.	mop	Past	yes	Al __mopped__ the eggshells from the deck.
The chef checks the shrimp on the grill.	check	Present progressive (right now)	no	The chef **is checking** the shrimp on the grill.
1. Chad flips the chops with tongs.		Past		Chad _____ the chops with tongs.
2. They stash their mesh tank tops in their backpacks.		Past		They _____ their mesh tank tops in their backpacks.
3. Hank sits on the bench next to the spring.		Present progressive		Hank _____ on the bench next to the spring.
4. Lin ships the gaskets and gas tanks to her shop.		Present progressive		Lin _____ the gaskets and gas tanks to her shop.
5. The insects chomp on the plants.		Past		The insects _____ on the plants.

Exercise 3 · Find It: Simple Predicate

▸ Find the simple predicate in each of these sentences.

▸ Underline each simple predicate.

▸ The first one is done for you, as an example.

1. They <u>chilled</u> the soft drinks.

2. She pitches in the last inning.

3. We sang there last spring.

4. His sister shopped for black pants.

5. Mr. Long rings the bell for class.

6. He chops things on this block.

7. We whipped the milk with the whisk.

8. Those men fished in the gulf.

9. The ship brings things that we can't send by air.

10. They scratched the desk.

Unit 8 · Lesson 2

Exercise 4 · Sort It: Present and Past Tense

▸ Reread each sentence in Exercise 3, **Find It: Simple Predicate**.

▸ Decide whether the simple predicate in each sentence is:

  • Present tense or

  • Past tense

▸ Write the underlined predicates in the correct column in the chart below.

▸ The first one is done for you.

▸ Use the **Tense Timeline** in the *Student Text*, page 44, as a guide.

Present Tense	Past Tense
	chilled

Exercise 5 · Combine It: Compound Subjects

▶ Combine these sentences into one sentence using the conjunction **and**.

▶ Write the sentence on the line.

▶ Circle both nouns in the compound subject.

1. Whales live in pods.   Dolphins live in pods.

_____

2. Squid are food for whales.   Fish are food for whales.

_____

3. Large ships stop for whales.   Small boats stop for whales.

_____

4. Squid are sifted in.   Plants are sifted in.

_____

5. Whales are fun to watch.   Dolphins are fun to watch.

_____

Unit 8 Lesson 3

Exercise 1 · Listening for Sounds in Words

▸ Listen for the sound / *ng* / in each word your teacher says.

▸ Write the letters **ng** in the box where you hear the sound / *ng* /.

▸ If you do not hear / *ng* /, write the letters for the word's sounds in the boxes.

1.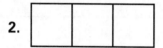

2.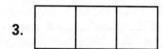

3.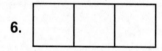

4.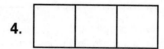

5.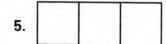

▸ Listen for the sound / *ch* / in each word your teacher says.

▸ Write the letters **ch** or **tch** in the box where you hear the sound / *ch* /.

▸ If you do not hear / *ch* /, write the letters for the word's sounds in the boxes.

6.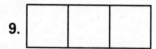

7.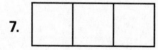

8.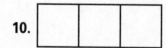

9.

10.

Exercise 2 · Add It: Using -es

▸ Read the words in each column.

▸ Look for the pattern in the words.

▸ Write the pattern in the blank. The first one is done for you.

Pattern: The words end with sh.	Pattern: _____ _____	Pattern: _____ _____
wish _____	rich _____	patch _____
flash _____	inch _____	hitch _____
cash _____	ranch _____	catch _____

▸ Add -es to each word above. Write the word in the blank.

▸ When do we use -es?

_____

_____

▸ How many syllables are in each of the words you wrote above after forming plural nouns or third person singular verbs with -es? _____

▸ What is another way to remember which plural nouns and third person singular verbs are spelled with -es?

_____

_____

_____

Unit 8 · Lesson 3

Exercise 3 · Find It: Essential Words

▸ Find the Unit 8 **Essential Words** in these sentences.

▸ Underline them. There may be more than one in a sentence.

1. How many classes do you have?

2. What was the movie about?

3. I don't have any lunch money.

4. We're going out to dinner.

5. Write each incorrect word five times.

▸ Write the **Essential Words** in the spaces.

_____   _____   _____

_____   _____   _____

▸ List the **Essential Word** pairs that rhyme.

_____   _____

_____   _____

Exercise 4 · Word Networks: Homophones

▸ Write the words **which** and **witch** on the lines in the Venn diagram.

▸ Fill in information about both words.

▸ Identify what is the same about the two words.

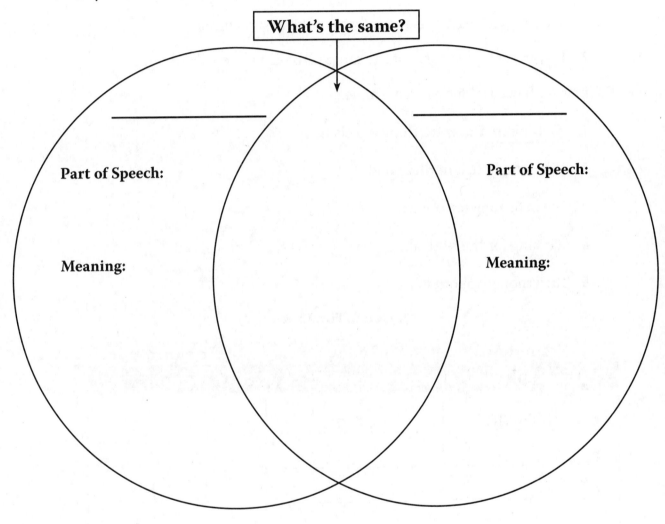

What's the same?

Part of Speech:

Meaning:

Part of Speech:

Meaning:

▸ Fill in the blanks below with **which** or **witch**.

1. _____ dog is yours?

2. I am going to the Halloween party as a _____ .

3. _____ of those houses do you live in?

4. _____ _____ has the best costume?.

Unit 8 · Lesson 3

Exercise 5 · Identify It: Irregular Past Tense Verbs

▶ Listen to the sentences as your teacher reads them.

▶ Identify and underline the simple predicate in each sentence.

▶ On the chart below, write:

    1. The irregular past tense verb form in the first column.

    2. The present tense form of the same verb in the second column.

▶ The first sentence is done as an example.

    1. We brought the extra things to class.

    2. They caught fish in that pond.

    3. The bells rang for class.

    4. We sang for the festival.

    5. They thought about it.

Tense Timeline

Yesterday	Today	Tomorrow
Irregular Past	Present	Future
1. brought	bring	
2 _____	_____	
3 _____	_____	
4 _____	_____	
5. _____	_____	

Exercise 6 · Use the Clues

▶ Use meaning signals to define the word **element**.

1. Underline the vocabulary word.

2. Read the text surrounding the unknown word.

3. Underline the words that define the unknown word.

4. Circle the meaning signals.

5. Put a double underline under examples of elements.

---

based on "Whale Song"

A whale's song has many parts. First, there is an *element*. An element is one sound. Elements can be long groans. They can be low moans. They can be roars. They can be trills. They can be cries. They can be snores. They can be growls, whistles, or chirps. Another part of a whale's song is a *phrase*. Elements repeat in patterns. Two to four different elements repeat. This makes a short sound string. We call the strings *phrases*.

▶ Write a definition based on the context clues.

element: _____

_____

▶ What are some examples of elements in a whale's song?

_____

_____

Exercise 7 · Answer It

▸ Underline the signal word.

▸ Answer each question in a complete sentence.

1. Repeat the *parts* of a whale song.

_____

_____

2. Retrieve information that tells *when* whales sing.

_____

_____

3. Recall the *gender* of the whale that sings.

_____

_____

4. Describe the *purposes* of whale song.

_____

_____

5. How do you recognize if a whale has changed its song?

_____

_____

▸ Write the letters for the last sound in each word your teacher says.

1. _____   2. _____   3. _____   4. _____   5. _____

6. _____   7. _____   8. _____   9. _____   10. _____

Unit 8 · Lesson 4

Exercise 2 · Identify It: Past or Present Progressive

▸ Read each sentence. Think about the **Tense Timeline**.

▸ Decide if the verb signals:

- • Past tense or

- • Present progressive

▸ Mark your choice by putting an X in the correct column.

Sentence	Past	Present Progressive
Examples: Beth is fixing the shelf in Chad's shack.		X
Hon passed the last quiz in math.	X	
They are clanging the bells on the 4th of July.		X
1. We are catching a lot of fish in the pond.		
2. Frank dashed to the exit.		
3. The chimp clenched the stick.		
4. Patrick dished up hotdogs at the picnic.		
5. Pedro is plugging the Elvis lamp into the outlet.		
6. Kim's chicks hatched in the spring.		
7. Beth and Chad are ringing bells and gongs in the band.		
8. Frank patched the rips in the tent.		
9. His songs filled the hall with swinging jazz.		
10. The song helped them during the contest.		

Exercise 3 · Rewrite It : Irregular Past Tense

▸ Do the first sentence with your teacher.

▸ Underline the present tense verb in the sentence. Think about its irregular past tense form.

▸ Write the sentence, changing the verb to past tense.

▸ Refer to the chart of irregular verbs in your *Student Text*, page 45, for spelling.

▸ Circle the irregular past tense verb after you write the sentence.

Present Tense	Past Tense (*irregular*)
1. I <u>think</u> about the math test.	I (thought) about the math test.
2. They catch a dozen fish.	_____
3. We bring the sandwiches.	_____
4. We sing in Mrs. Ming's class.	_____
5. The bells ring.	_____

Unit 8 · Lesson 4

Exercise 4 · Blueprint for Reading: Transition Words and Details

▶ Circle the transition words: **First**, **another**, **the last**.

▶ Highlight in blue the remaining words in the sentences that start with the transition words.

**"Parts of the Song" section
from "Whale Song"**

A whale's song has many parts. First, there is an *element*. An *element* is one sound. *Elements* can be long groans. They can be low moans. They can be roars. They can be trills. They can be cries. They can be snores. They can be growls, whistles, or chirps. Another part of a whale's song is a *phrase*. *Elements* repeat in patterns. Two to four different *elements* repeat. This makes a short sound string. We call the strings *phrases*. The last part of a whale's song is the *theme*. Whales repeat *phrases* several times. A set of similar *phrases* is a *theme*. Whales sing from one *theme* to the next. They do not pause.

Exercise 1 · Say and Write

‣ Repeat the sound your teacher says.

‣ Write the letter or letters for each sound.

‣ Add the correct diacritical mark (breve) over the vowel letter to signal the short vowel sound.

1. _____   2. _____   3. _____   4. _____   5. _____

6. _____   7. _____   8. _____   9. _____   10. _____

Exercise 2 · Sort It: Consonant Digraphs

‣ Read the words in the box.

‣ Sort the words according to the sound of the consonant digraph.

‣ Write the words under the correct column heading.

‣ Some words belong in more than one column.

| fish | thank | bang | ship | match | this | rich | without |
| which | them | when | thing | that | chick | wish | bath |

/ ch /	/ sh /	voiceless / th /	voiced / th /	/ hw /	/ ng /

‣ Circle the words with a voiced / th /.

‣ Say the circled words and feel the vibration in your throat.

Exercise 1 · Spelling Pretest 2

▶ Write the words your teacher repeats.

1. _____
2. _____
3. _____
4. _____
5. _____

6. _____
7. _____
8. _____
9. _____
10. _____

11. _____
12. _____
13. _____
14. _____
15. _____

Unit 8 · Lesson 6

Exercise 2 · Sort It: Meaning Categories

▸ Read the words in the box.

bang	chant	ring
honk	chat	chit chat
sing	gong	ding dong
clang	tell	crash
yell	call	bash

▸ Sort the words into categories.

Noises	Language

▸ Think of more words for each category.

Exercise 3 · Phrase It

▶ Use the penciling strategy to "scoop" the phrases in each sentence.

▶ Read the sentences as you would speak them.

▶ The first two are done for you.

1. Woody's treks prompted his songs.

2. This vast land impressed him.

3. He was thinking of the land's riches.

4. He wrote "This Land is Your Land."

5. The song expressed his thinking.

6. His songs have had an impact.

7. Woody kept writing songs.

8. His illness left him helpless.

9. Songs are his lasting gift.

10. We still sing them.

Unit 8 · Lesson 6

Exercise 4 · Find It: Consonant Digraphs

▶ Read the selection silently or quietly to yourself.

▶ Highlight or underline words with consonant digraphs.

---

from "A Man and His Songs"

Woody's treks prompted his songs. This vast land impressed him. He was thinking of the grand hills. He was thinking of the land's riches. He wrote "This Land Is Your Land." The song expressed his thinking. It was a big hit then. It is still a hit. He wrote many songs. His songs have had an impact.

▶ List five words with three different consonant digraphs on the lines below.

1. _____

2. _____

3. _____

4. _____

5. _____

Exercise 5 · Combine It: Compound Predicates

▸ Combine these sentences using the conjunction **and**.

▸ Circle both predicates in the sentence you write.

1. Woody Guthrie wrote songs. Woody Guthrie played the guitar.

_____

2. Woody drilled wells. Woody picked crops.

_____

3. He drifted from job to job. He sang for a living.

_____

4. They were singing all the way. They were playing all the way.

_____

5. He began spinning tales. He began telling stories.

_____

Exercise 1 · Add It: Using -es

▸ Read each word in the first column.

▸ Say each word in its plural (noun) or third person singular present tense (verb) form.

▸ Listen to how it sounds.

▸ Write the number of syllables you hear in the second column.

▸ Write the plural word in either the third or fourth column.

▸ The first one is done for you.

Word	Say the plural noun or third person singular present tense verb. Is it **one** or **two** syllables?	If you hear **one** syllable, add ~s.	If you hear **two** syllables, add ~es.
fox	2		foxes
witch			
bath			
rich			
dish			
sink			
king			
pass			
whiz			
shop			

(continued)

Exercise 1 (continued) · Add It: Using -es

▸ When do we use **-es**?

_____

▸ What happens when we add **-es** to make a plural noun or a third person singular present tense verb?

_____

_____

_____

Unit 8 · Lesson 7

Exercise 2 · Identify It: Past Tense

▶ Read each sentence.

▶ Underline the past tense verb.

▶ Mark the correct column to show if the **-ed** sounds like / *t* /, / *d* /, or / *ĭd* /.

▶ Mark your choice by putting an X in the correct column.

Sentence	-ed sounds like / *t* /	-ed sounds like / *d* /	-ed sounds like / *ĭd* /
Examples: I <u>winked</u> at her from the dock.	X		
The humpback whale <u>nabbed</u> the fish.		X	
He <u>lifted</u> the chest out of the ship.			X
1. Roger spotted the whales migrating in the spring.			
2. A whale banged into the hull of his ship.			
3. Roger intended to inspect his ship before the trip.			
4. He checked the hull to find out if anything was wrong.			
5. Roger scratched his hand inspecting the ship's mast.			
6. With an odd grin, Roger dashed into the cabin.			
7. Roger patched his hand.			
8. Roger's dog Fang smelled clams on the ship's deck.			
9. Roger sprinted out of the cabin when the whales swam back.			
10. Fang crashed into Roger as he shot past.			

Exercise 3 · Sentence Dictation

▶ Listen to your teacher dictate the sentence pairs.

▶ Write both sentences on the first set of lines.

▶ Circle the complete predicate in each sentence.

▶ Combine the predicates to create a compound predicate with the conjunction **and**.

▶ Write the combined sentence on the next line, under the sentence pair.

1. Woody's dad (lost his job.)   Woody's dad (left.)
Woody's dad lost his job and left.

2. _____   _____

_____

3. _____   _____

_____

4. _____   _____

_____

5. _____   _____

_____

Unit 8 · Lesson 7

Exercise 4 · Find It: Compound Predicates

▸ Review the compound predicate sentences you wrote in Exercise 3, **Sentence Dictation**.

▸ Write the two simple predicates in each sentence, compounded by **and**, on the lines below.

▸ The first one is done as an example.

1. lost and left _____

2. _____

3. _____

4. _____

5. _____

Exercise 1 · Syllable Awareness: Segmentation

▸ Listen to each word your teacher says.

▸ Repeat the word.

▸ Write the number of syllables in the word.

▸ Write the letter for each vowel sound you hear in the word.

▸ Add the correct diacritical mark (breve) over the vowel letters to signal the short vowel sounds.

	How many syllables do you hear?	First Vowel Sound	Second Vowel Sound	Third Vowel Sound
1.				
2.				
3.				
4.				
5.				
6.				
7.				
8.				
9.				
10.				

Unit 8 · Lesson 8

Exercise 2 · Listening for Word Parts

▸ Listen to each word.

▸ Write the word part that your teacher repeats.

1. _____   2. _____   3. _____   4. _____   5. _____

6. _____   7. _____   8. _____   9. _____   10. _____

Exercise 3 · Sort It: Consonant Digraphs

▸ Sort the word parts from Exercise 2, **Listening for Word Parts**, according to their consonant digraphs.

▸ Some words may be used more than once.

▸ Label the sorted words.

Exercise 4 · Word Networks: Antonyms

▸ Read the words in the **Word Bank**.

▸ Write the antonym (opposite) for the word your teacher says.

Word Bank

rich	king
summer	long
pitch	strong
catch	bring
thick	sink

1. take _____
2. throw _____
3. queen _____
4. short _____
5. poor _____

6. float _____
7. winter _____
8. weak _____
9. thin _____
10. catch _____

Unit 8 · Lesson 8

Exercise 5 · Diagram It: Subject + Compound Predicate

▸ Read each sentence.

▸ Diagram each sentence.

▸ Place an **X** over the **vertical line** that cuts through and separates

- The complete subject and

- The complete predicate.

▸ Be careful to show the compound predicate in each sentence.

1. Woody drifted and did odd jobs.

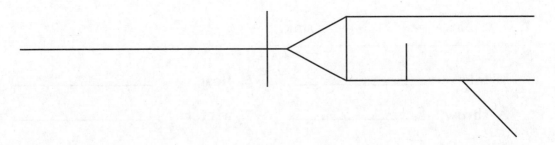

2. Woody's dad lost his job and left.

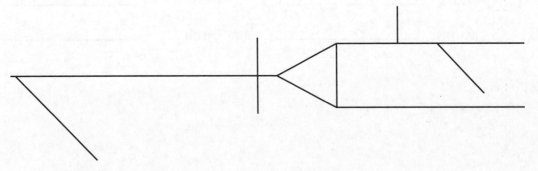

3. He picked and harvested crops.

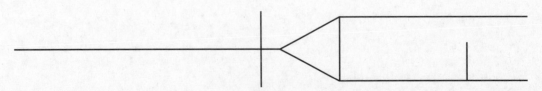

(continued)

4. Woody worked and sang his songs.

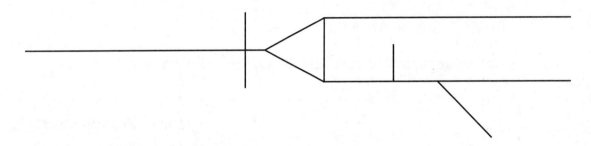

5. He wrote and published "This Land Is Your Land."

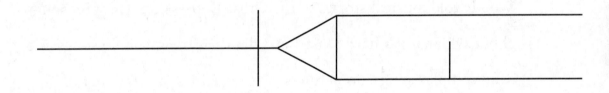

Unit 8 · Lesson 8

Exercise 6 · Use the Clues

▸ Use word substitutions to define the word **spinning**.

- • Circle the vocabulary word.

- • Read text surrounding the unknown word.

- • Underline the words that help define the unknown word.

---

from "Woody's Song"

At 17, Woody discovered the guitar. It was like magic! He began spinning musical tales.

Woody told musical stories of the Great Depression. He spun songs about Oklahoma's hard Dust Bowl days. He sang simple songs. He sang complex songs. Sometimes, he sang silly songs for kids.

▸ Write a definition based on the context clues. Verify your definition with the dictionary or www.yourdictionary.com.

 spinning: _____

Exercise 7 · Answer It

▸ Read each question.

▸ Underline the signal word in each question.

▸ Answer each question in a **complete sentence**.

▸ Use part of the question to help you write the answer.

1. Who was Woody Guthrie?

_____

_____

2. What did he do?

_____

_____

_____

3. When was Woody born? When did he die?

_____

_____

4. Where did Woody grow up? Where did he raise his family?

_____

_____

5. What did Nora's descriptions tell about Woody as a father?

_____

_____

Exercise 1 · Listening for Sounds in Words

▸ Write the letter or letters for the last sound in each word your teacher says.

1. _____   2. _____   3. _____   4. _____   5. _____

6. _____   7. _____   8. _____   9. _____   10. _____

Exercise 2 · Syllable Awareness: Segmentation

▸ Listen to each word your teacher says.

▸ Repeat the word.

▸ Write the number of syllables in the word.

▸ Write the letter for each vowel sound you hear in the word.

▸ Add the correct diacritical mark (breve) over the vowel letters to signal the short vowel sounds.

	How many syllables do you hear?	First Vowel Sound	Second Vowel Sound	Third Vowel Sound
1.				
2.				
3.				
4.				
5.				
6.				
7.				
8.				
9.				
10.				

Unit 8 · Lesson 9

Exercise 3 · Sentence Dictation

▸ Listen to each sentence.

▸ Repeat the sentence.

▸ Write it on the line.

1. _____

2. _____

3. _____

4. _____

5. _____

▸ Read sentences 1, 2, and 3.

▸ Find the words that follow the **1 - 1 - 1** rule.

▸ Write them on the line.

_____

▸ Read sentences 4 and 5.

▸ Find the rhyming words.

▸ Write them on the line.

_____

Exercise 4 · Choose It and Use It: Verb Phrases

▸ Read the words and phrases in the **Word Bank.**

▸ Read the whole story with the empty blanks first.

▸ Select the best word or phrase from the **Word Bank** to fill in each blank and complete the sentences.

▸ Some words or phrases may fit into two blanks, but each word or phrase fits better into only one blank.

Word Bank

1. picked	**8.** will help
2. will pick	**9.** passed
3. is helping	**10.** is studying
4. went	**11.** chatted
5. lived	**12.** is adding
6. is thinking	**13.** expected
7. mixed	

(continued)

Exercise 4 (continued) · Choose It and Use It: Verb Phrases

"David Ho: 'Man of the Year'"

David Ho _____ in a small town in China. His dad left for America when David was still a kid. The family sent letters back and forth and _____ on the phone. They all _____ to go to America.

At last they all _____ to America.

School was very hard for David. He _____ few tests. He did not know English. He felt bad, but he didn't give up. He said that he _____ up English. At last he _____ up a lot of English.

Now he _____ a lot of people. He is a doctor. He _____ a lot to life. He _____ about AIDS. He wants to bring an end to AIDS and _____ it in his lab.

He _____ new pills. The new pills helped people. In 1996, *Time* magazine made David Ho "Man of the Year." A boy from China became a famous doctor in America. He says he _____ people for as long as he can.

Exercise 5 · Sentence Dictation

▶ Write the sentences your teacher dictates.

1. _____

_____

_____

2. _____

_____

_____

3. _____

_____

_____

4. _____

_____

_____

5. _____

_____

_____

Unit 8 · Lesson 9

Exercise 6 · Take Note

Note-taking Guide	
Topic (**What was the article or program about?**)	_____ _____
Who or what?	_____
What happened?	_____ _____ _____
When?	_____
Where?	_____ _____
Outcome or impact?	_____ _____
Why important?	_____ _____

Summary
_____   _____   _____   _____

Exercise 1 · Listening for Sounds in Words

▸ Write the letters for the sounds in each word your teacher says.

▸ Circle the words with the / *ch* / sound at the end.

▸ Draw a box around the words with the / *hw* / sound at the beginning.

1. □ □ □

2. □ □ □

3. □ □ □

4. □ □ □

5. □ □ □

6. □ □ □

7. □ □ □ □

8. □ □ □ □

9. □ □ □

10. □ □ □ □

Unit 8 · Lesson 10

Exercise 2 · Sort It: Meaning Categories

▸ Follow along as your teacher reads parts of "**Woody's Song**."

▸ Listen for words that name people, stringed instruments, or furniture. Underline them when you hear them.

▸ Sort the words into the categories.

from "Woody's Song"

Woody's daughter, Nora, has many fond memories of her father and his music. "Music—the guitar, the fiddle, the mandolin—was as much a part of our household as the couch, the bed, or the chair," she explained. "We really lived with all the music, all this art. It wasn't like they were something precious on the shelf, something you never touched. You know, he'd write a song and it would sit on our table. You might have chocolate milk, and it might spill, and there might be these little stains."

People	Stringed Instruments	Furniture

What pronouns refer to people? _____

Check off the activities you complete with each lesson. Evaluate your accomplishments at the end of each lesson. Pay attention to teacher evaluations and comments.

Unit Objectives	Lesson 1 (Date:_____)	Lesson 2 (Date:_____)
STEP 1 **Phonemic Awareness and Phonics** • Say the sounds for the vowel **u** (/ ŭ / and / o͞o /). • Write the letter for the sound / ŭ / and the sound / o͞o / as in **book**. • Use the diacritical mark, breve, to signal the short vowel sound.	❑ Move It and Mark it ❑ Phonemic Drills ❑ See and Say ❑ Exercise 1: Say and Write ❑ Handwriting Practice ❑ Exercise 2: Listening for Sounds in Words	❑ Vowel Chart (T) ❑ Phonemic Drills ❑ Exercise 1: Say and Write ❑ See and Say
STEP 2 **Word Recognition and Spelling** • Read and spell words with sound-spelling correspondences from this and previous units. • Read and spell contractions with **would**. • Read and spell **Essential Words:** *been, could, should, too, two, would.* • Read and spell compound words.	❑ Exercise 3: Spelling Pretest 1 ❑ Build It, Bank It ❑ Memorize It	❑ Build It, Bank It ❑ Word Fluency 1 ❑ Memorize It ❑ Handwriting Practice
STEP 3 **Vocabulary and Morphology** • Define **Unit Vocabulary** words. • Identify and generate antonyms, synonyms, and homophones.	❑ Unit Vocabulary ❑ Multiple Meaning Map (T) ❑ Expression of the Day	❑ Exercise 2: Find It: Plurals ❑ Exercise 3: Add It: Plurals ❑ Expression of the Day
STEP 4 **Grammar and Usage** • Identify verb phrases (HV + MV). • Identify and write past progressive verbs. • Write irregular past tense verbs. • Combine direct objects to form a compound direct object.	❑ Exercise 4: Rewrite It: Present Progressive	❑ Introduce: Past Progressive ❑ Exercise 4: Rewrite It: Past Progressive ❑ Exercise 5: Sort It: Past or Present
STEP 5 **Listening and Reading Comprehension** • Read with inflection, phrasing, and expression. • Identify signal words for comprehension. • Identify transition words in informational text. • Use context clues to define words.	❑ Exercise 5: Phrase It ❑ Decodable Text: "Bugs Live!" ❑ Exercise 6: Find It: Words With / ŭ /	❑ Exercise 6: Find It: Words With / ŭ / (Lesson 1) ❑ Passage Fluency 1
STEP 6 **Speaking and Writing** • Use transition words for classification in paragraph development. • Organize information to write from text material using a graphic organizer. • Use signal words to answer questions.	❑ Masterpiece Sentences: Stages 1–3 ❑ Sentence Types: Fact or Opinion?	❑ Exercise 6: Rewrite It: Compound Sentence Parts
Self-Evaluation (5 is the highest) **Effort** = I produced my best work. **Participation** = I was actively involved in tasks. **Independence** = I worked on my own.	Effort: 1 2 3 4 5 Participation: 1 2 3 4 5 Independence: 1 2 3 4 5	Effort: 1 2 3 4 5 Participation: 1 2 3 4 5 Independence: 1 2 3 4 5
Teacher Evaluation	Effort: 1 2 3 4 5 Participation: 1 2 3 4 5 Independence: 1 2 3 4 5	Effort: 1 2 3 4 5 Participation: 1 2 3 4 5 Independence: 1 2 3 4 5

Lesson 3 (Date:_____)	Lesson 4 (Date:_____)	Lesson 5 (Date:_____)
❏ Vowel Chart (T) ❏ Phonemic Drills ❏ Exercise 1: Listening for Sounds in Words	❏ Vowel Chart (T) ❏ Phonemic Drills ❏ Exercise 1: Listening for Sounds in Words ❏ Letter-Sound Fluency	❏ Phonemic Drills ❏ Letter-Sound Fluency ❏ Exercise 1: Say and Write ❏ Content Mastery: Sound-Spelling Correspondences
❏ Exercise 2: Sort It: Sounds for <u>u</u> ❏ Exercise 3: Add It: Plurals ❏ Word Fluency 1 ❏ Exercise 4: Find It: Essential Words	❏ Exercise 2: Sort It: / ŭ / for <u>o</u> ❏ Word Fluency 2 ❏ Type It ❏ Handwriting Practice	❏ Content Mastery: Spelling Posttest 1 ❏ Exercise 2: Sort It: Vowel Sounds
❏ Exercise 5: Word Networks: Homophones ❏ Draw It: Idioms ❏ Expression of the Day	❏ Exercise 3: Find It: Possessives ❏ Exercise 4: Choose It and Use It ❏ Expression of the Day	❏ Multiple Meaning Map (T) ❏ Expression of the Day
❏ Exercise 6: Identify It: Past Tense ❏ Exercise 7: Sort It: Regular and Irregular Verbs	❏ Using the Tense Timeline (T) ❏ Exercise 5: Rewrite It: Present Progressive to Past Progressive	❏ Masterpiece Sentences: Stages 1–6 ❏ Using Masterpiece Sentences: Changing Past to Past Progressive
❏ Instructional Text: "How Bugs Bug Us" ❏ Exercise 8: Use the Clues	❏ Exercise 6: Blueprint for Reading: Main Ideas and Transition Words (T)	❏ Exercise 6: Blueprint for Reading: Identifying the Details (Lesson 4)
❏ Exercise 9: Answer It	❏ Blueprint for Reading: Main Ideas and Transition Words (T) ❏ Challenge Text: "Buggy English"	❏ Blueprint for Writing: Details (T) ❏ Write It: Summary Paragraph (T) ❏ Challenge Text: "Buggy English"
Effort: 1 2 3 4 5 **Participation:** 1 2 3 4 5 **Independence:** 1 2 3 4 5	**Effort:** 1 2 3 4 5 **Participation:** 1 2 3 4 5 **Independence:** 1 2 3 4 5	**Effort:** 1 2 3 4 5 **Participation:** 1 2 3 4 5 **Independence:** 1 2 3 4 5
Effort: 1 2 3 4 5 **Participation:** 1 2 3 4 5 **Independence:** 1 2 3 4 5	**Effort:** 1 2 3 4 5 **Participation:** 1 2 3 4 5 **Independence:** 1 2 3 4 5	**Effort:** 1 2 3 4 5 **Participation:** 1 2 3 4 5 **Independence:** 1 2 3 4 5

Check off the activities you complete with each lesson. Evaluate your accomplishments at the end of each lesson. Pay attention to teacher evaluations and comments.

Unit Objectives	Lesson 6 (Date:_____)	Lesson 7 (Date:_____)
STEP 1 — **Phonemic Awareness and Phonics** • Say the sounds for the vowel <u>u</u> (/ ŭ / and / ŏŏ /). • Write the letter for the sound / ŭ / and the sound / ŏŏ / as in book. • Use the diacritical mark, breve, to signal the short vowel sound.	❑ Phonemic Drills ❑ Move It and Mark It ❑ See and Say ❑ Handwriting Practice ❑ Syllable Segmentation	❑ Phonemic Drills ❑ See and Name ❑ Name and Write ❑ Syllable Deletion
STEP 2 — **Word Recognition and Spelling** • Read and spell words with sound-spelling correspondences from this and previous units. • Read and spell contractions with **would**. • Read and spell the **Essential Words**: *been, could, should, too, two, would*. • Read and spell compound words.	❑ Exercise 1: Spelling Pretest 2 ❑ Build It, Bank It ❑ Word Fluency 3	❑ Contractions ❑ Exercise 1: Contract It ❑ Double It (T)
STEP 3 — **Vocabulary and Morphology** • Define **Unit Vocabulary** words. • Identify and generate antonyms, synonyms, and homophones.	❑ More About Compound Words ❑ Unit Vocabulary ❑ Exercise 2: Sort It: Word Meanings ❑ Expression of the Day	❑ Exercise 2: Choose It and Use It: Singular or Plural ❑ Exercise 3: Rewrite It: Suffixes With **-s** ❑ Expression of the Day
STEP 4 — **Grammar and Usage** • Identify verb phrases (HV + MV). • Identify and write past progressive verbs. • Write irregular past tense verbs. • Combine direct objects to form a compound direct object.	❑ Compound Direct Objects ❑ Exercise 3: Combine It: Direct Objects	❑ Exercise 4: Expand It: Direct Objects
STEP 5 — **Listening and Reading Comprehension** • Read with inflection, phrasing, and expression. • Identify signal words for comprehension. • Identify transition words in informational text. • Use context clues to define words.	❑ Exercise 4: Phrase It ❑ Decodable Text: "Bad Bugs" ❑ Exercise 5: Find It: Words With / ŭ /	❑ Exercise 5: Find It: Words With / ŭ / ❑ Passage Fluency 2
STEP 6 — **Speaking and Writing** • Use transition words for classification in paragraph development. • Organize information to write from text material using a graphic organizer. • Use signal words to answer questions.	❑ Masterpiece Sentences: Stages 1 and 2 ❑ Using Masterpiece Sentences: Compound Direct Objects	❑ Exercise 5: Combine It: Direct Objects
Self-Evaluation (5 is the highest) **Effort** = I produced my best work. **Participation** = I was actively involved in tasks. **Independence** = I worked on my own.	Effort: 1 2 3 4 5 Participation: 1 2 3 4 5 Independence: 1 2 3 4 5	Effort: 1 2 3 4 5 Participation: 1 2 3 4 5 Independence: 1 2 3 4 5
Teacher Evaluation	Effort: 1 2 3 4 5 Participation: 1 2 3 4 5 Independence: 1 2 3 4 5	Effort: 1 2 3 4 5 Participation: 1 2 3 4 5 Independence: 1 2 3 4 5

Lesson 8 (Date:_____)	**Lesson 9** (Date:_____)	**Lesson 10** (Date:_____)
❑ Phonemic Drills ❑ Letter-Name Fluency ❑ Exercise 1: Syllable Awareness: Segmentation	❑ Phonemic Drills ❑ Exercise 1: Listening for Sounds in Words ❑ Letter-Name Fluency ❑ Exercise 2: Syllable Awareness: Segmentation	❑ Exercise 1: Listening for Sounds in Words
❑ Exercise 2: Listening for Word Parts ❑ Exercise 3: Sort It: Vowel Sounds ❑ Word Fluency 4	❑ Exercise 3: Sentence Dictation	❑ Content Mastery: Spelling Posttest 2
❑ Exercise 4: Word Networks: Antonyms, Synonyms, and Attributes ❑ Content Mastery: Word Meanings	❑ Exercise 4: Find It: Plural Noun Endings ❑ Expression of the Day	❑ Exercise 2: Sort It: Word Meanings ❑ Exercise 3: Define It ❑ Draw It: Idioms ❑ Expression of the Day
❑ Exercise 5: Diagram It: Compound Direct Objects (T)	❑ Masterpiece Sentences: Stages 1 and 2 ❑ Using Masterpiece Sentences: Compound Direct Objects	❑ Content Mastery: Sentence Structure/Verbs
❑ Instructional Text: "New Old Insects" ❑ Exercise 6: Use the Clues	❑ Exercise 5: Information: Fact or Opinion?	❑ Content Mastery: Answering Questions ❑ Instructional Text: "New Old Insects"
❑ Exercise 7: Answer It	❑ Exercise 6: Take Note (T) ❑ Challenge Text: "Lighting Bugs"	❑ Exercise 6: Take Note (T) (Lesson 9) ❑ Write It: Summary Paragraph (T) ❑ Challenge Text: "Lighting Bugs"
Effort: 1 2 3 4 5 **Participation:** 1 2 3 4 5 **Independence:** 1 2 3 4 5	**Effort:** 1 2 3 4 5 **Participation:** 1 2 3 4 5 **Independence:** 1 2 3 4 5	**Effort:** 1 2 3 4 5 **Participation:** 1 2 3 4 5 **Independence:** 1 2 3 4 5
Effort: 1 2 3 4 5 **Participation:** 1 2 3 4 5 **Independence:** 1 2 3 4 5	**Effort:** 1 2 3 4 5 **Participation:** 1 2 3 4 5 **Independence:** 1 2 3 4 5	**Effort:** 1 2 3 4 5 **Participation:** 1 2 3 4 5 **Independence:** 1 2 3 4 5

Exercise 1 · Say and Write

▸ Say each sound your teacher says.

▸ Write the letter or letters as you say the sound.

▸ Add the correct diacritical mark (breve) over the vowel letter to signal the short vowel sound.

1. _____   2. _____   3. _____   4. _____   5. _____

6. _____   7. _____   8. _____   9. _____   10. _____

Exercise 2 · Listening for Sounds in Words

▸ Listen for the vowel sounds / ŭ /, / ă /, / ĭ /, / ŏ /, or / ĕ / in the words your teacher says.

▸ Write the letter for the vowel sound in the box that shows where you hear it.

▸ Add the proper diacritical mark (breve) over the vowel letter to signal the short vowel sound. Put the breve (˘) over the vowel.

1.
2.
3.
4.
5.

6.
7.
8.
9.
10.

Exercise 3 · Spelling Pretest 1

▶ Write the words your teacher says.

1. _____   6. _____   11. _____

2. _____   7. _____   12. _____

3. _____   8. _____   13. _____

4. _____   9. _____   14. _____

5. _____   10. _____   15. _____

Exercise 4 · Rewrite It: Present Progressive

▶ Read each sentence.

▶ Underline the predicate once.

▶ Restate the sentence in the present progressive.

▶ Write the new predicate on the line at right.

▶ See the first one as an example.

1. We <u>discuss</u> these problems.   _are discussing_

2. They slump on the steps.   _____

3. They brush off their desks.   _____

4. She instructs us in math.   _____

5. I rush to get there.   _____

6. He publishes our work.   _____

7. She hunts for facts.   _____

8. They fund this project.   _____

9. The chinch bug cuts into the plants.   _____

10. The bed bug jumps on your bed!   _____

Unit 9 · Lesson 1

Exercise 5 · Phrase It

▸ Use the penciling strategy to "scoop" the phrases in each sentence.

▸ Read as you would speak them.

▸ The first two are done for you.

1. A bug's body has three segments.

2. Our bodies do not have three segments.

3. Our bodies do not have six legs.

4. Your body has lots of bugs on it.

5. In fact, some bugs love to live on your body!

6. Some bugs love plants, too.

7. Some bugs live on pets.

8. Some bugs love living in beds.

9. You cannot spot a dust mite with your eyes.

10. Some of us get sick from this bug.

Exercise 6 · Find It: Words With / ŭ /

▸ Read the text quietly to yourself.

▸ Highlight or underline words with / ŭ /.

▸ List five words from the text with / ŭ / on the lines below the reading.

Hint: / ŭ / can be spelled with **o** in some words.

---

from "Bugs Live!"

We fluff the blankets on the bed. Then our eyes get red. We dust the top of the desk. Then our eyes itch. What is happening? Bugs are bugging us. It is not the dust. It's the bugs! To be exact, dust mites are bugging us. You cannot spot a dust mite with your eyes. It is too small. Dust mites live on skin cells that we shed. Some of us get sick from this bug.

---

1. _____

2. _____

3. _____

4. _____

5. _____

Exercise 1 · Say and Write

▸ Say the sound your teacher says.

▸ Write the letter or letters for each sound.

1. _____   2. _____   3. _____   4. _____   5. _____

6. _____   7. _____   8. _____   9. _____   10. _____

Exercise 2 · Find It: Plurals

▸ Read each sentence.

▸ Underline the plural noun in each sentence.

1. Hank dumped the ashes into the trash.

2. The suspect ran to the shacks by the pond.

3. Pancho put his sketches in the attic.

4. Sam picked the slugs off the plant.

5. Chico scratched the rashes on his leg.

Exercise 3 · Add It: Plurals

▸ Read each singular noun.

▸ Put an X in the column that describes the noun.

▸ Write the plural of the noun.

▸ Read the plural noun to a peer.

Singular Noun	Ends in s, z, x, ch, sh, or tch: Add -es for the plural.	Ends in any other letters: Add -s for the plural.	Plural Noun
Examples: inch	X		inches
clump		X	clumps
1. fox			
2. crash			
3. bulb			
4. rank			
5. crutch			
6. punch			
7. pulpit			
8. brush			
9. switch			
10. suffix			

Unit 9 · Lesson 2

Exercise 4 · Rewrite It: Past Progressive

▸ Read the sentence.

▸ Underline the present progressive predicate.

▸ Restate the sentence with a past progressive predicate.

▸ Rewrite the verb phrase as past progressive on the lines at the right.

1. We <u>are discussing</u> these problems.   <u>were discussing</u>

2. They are slumping on the steps.   _____

3. They are brushing off their desks.   _____

4. She is instructing us in math.   _____

5. I am rushing to get there.   _____

6. He is publishing our work.   _____

7. She is hunting for facts.   _____

8. They are funding this project.   _____

9. The chinch bug is cutting into the plants.   _____

10. The bed bug is jumping on your bed!   _____

Exercise 5 · Sort It: Past or Present

▸ Read the verbs and verb phrases in the box below.

▸ Sort them into the correct column.

bluffed	is cutting	pushes	blushes	was drumming
is blushing	were brushing	flunked	rushes	was bumping
instructed	are scrubbing	bumps	hunted	were scrubbing

← ◀ **past** ━━━━━━━ **present** ━━━━━━━ **future** ▶ →

Past or Past Progressive	Present or Present Progressive
bluffed	

Unit 9 · Lesson 2

Exercise 6 · Rewrite It: Compound Sentence Parts

▸ Separate the combined sentence into two sentences.

▸ Identify whether the sentence has a compound subject or compound predicate.

▸ Underline your choice.

1. The class pushed and shoved.

compound subject

compound predicate

_____

2. The chipmunk and skunk are running.

compound subject

compound predicate

_____

3. The chipmunk and skunk ran into the sunlit bushes.

compound subject

compound predicate

_____

4. Lice lay eggs and spread quickly.

compound subject

compound predicate

_____

5. Pets and people are homes for bugs.

compound subject

compound predicate

_____

Exercise 1 · Listening for Sounds in Words

▸ Put an /ŭ/ where you hear the sound /ŭ/ in the words your teacher says.

▸ Put an /ŏŏ/ where you hear the sound /ŏŏ/.

1.

6.

2.

7.

3.

8.

4.

9.

5.

10.

Unit 9 · Lesson 3

Exercise 2 · Sort It: Sounds for u

▶ Use the vocabulary in the **Word Bank** below.

Word Bank

bull	rush	plush	push	much	lunch	put	run
bush	such	full	buzz	pull	cut	hull	brush

▶ Sort the words in the template according to their vowel sound.

▶ Write the word in the correct column.

u = / ŭ / as in rush	u = / ŏo / as in bush

1. Do **rush** and **bush** rhyme? Why or why not?

   _____

   _____

2. Find rhyming pairs or triplets in the **Word Bank**.

   _____

   _____

Exercise 3 · Add It: Plurals

▸ Read the words in the first column. All of them can be nouns.

▸ Say each word in its plural form. Decide if the plural has one or two syllables.

▸ Write the plural word in the correct column.

▸ Circle the words that can also be verbs.

Note: Adding **-s** or **-es** to a verb makes it third person singular, present tense.

Word	Say the plural. Think: Is it **one** or **two** syllables?	If **one** syllable, add -s	If **two** syllables, add -es
bush	2		bushes
hull			
bull			
lunch			
cut			
run			
brush			
hunch			
trunk			
rush			

When do we use **-es**?

_____

_____

_____

Exercise 4 · Find It: Essential Words

▸ Find the Unit 9 **Essential Words** in these sentences.

▸ Underline them. (There may be more than one in a sentence.)

1. Would you like help with that?

2. We could call your mom.

3. That costs too much money.

4. I have two tickets for you.

5. I should have been in the club.

▸ Write the **Essential Words** on the lines.

▸ Circle the three **Essential Words** that rhyme.

_____   _____   _____

_____   _____   _____

Exercise 5 · Word Networks: Homophones

▸ Write the words **two** and **too** on the lines in the Venn diagram.

▸ Fill in information about both words.

▸ Identify what is the same about the two words.

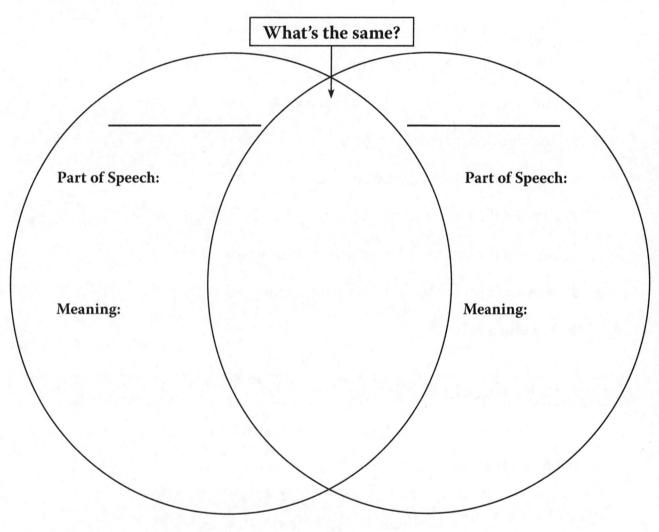

What's the same?

Part of Speech:

Meaning:

Part of Speech:

Meaning:

▸ Fill in the blanks with **two** or **too**.

1. May I have _____ pieces of pizza?

2. I want to go to the store _____ .

3. I have _____ much homework.

4. We saw _____ movies, _____ !

Unit 9 · Lesson 3

Exercise 6 · Identify It: Past Tense

▸ Underline the regular past tense verbs in the sentences below.

▸ Circle the irregular past tense verbs.

1. Ms. Ross (went) to the lab for her project.

2. We <u>hunted</u> for chinch bugs.

3. We had a film about chinch bugs.

4. The chinch bugs' eggs hatched in the grass.

5. The chinch bugs killed the grass.

6. We wrote a chinch bug project in class.

7. Kim did the project with me.

8. Ms. Ross helped the class with their chinch bug projects.

9. Kim and I got to class with our chinch bug project.

10. We won a ribbon!

Exercise 7 · Sort It: Regular and Irregular Verbs

▸ Use the past tense verbs you circled and underlined in Exercise 6.

▸ Sort them into the chart below.

Regular Past Tense Verbs (end in -ed)	Irregular Past Tense Verbs
hunted	went

Exercise 8 · Use the Clues

▸ Underline the vocabulary word **sebum**.

▸ Read the text surrounding the unknown word.

▸ Underline the words that help define the unknown word.

▸ Circle the meaning signal.

▸ Write a definition based on the context clues.

▸ Verify your definition with a dictionary or www.yourdictionary.com.

> **from "How Bugs Bug Us"**
>
> Eyelash mites are the final type of bug that exists on our body. You have mites in your eyelashes. Don't worry; they're harmless. These tiny bugs cling to eyelashes with eight tiny legs. They live on sebum, which is a natural oil in skin and hair. The truth is, lots of bugs just love our skin and hair!

Define It: Sebum- _____

_____

Unit 9 · Lesson 3

Exercise 9 · Answer It

▸ Answer each question in a complete sentence.

1. **Tell** how dust mites can make us sick.

   _____

   _____

2. **Define** the word *bacteria* in your own words.

   _____

   _____

3. **Predict** what could happen if one student comes to class with lice.

   _____

   _____

4. What do you **conclude** about the effect of eyelash mites?

   _____

   _____

5. **Illustrate** one type of bug that bugs us. Be sure to label the illustration.

   _____

   _____

Lesson 4

Exercise 1 · Listening for Sounds in Words

▸ Listen as your teacher says each word in the first column.

▸ Put an X in the column to show which vowel sound you hear.

	/ ŭ /	/ o͝o /
1. fun		
2. come		
3. rug		
4. full		
5. put		
6. bush		
7. month		
8. swung		
9. ton		
10. push		

Unit 9 · Lesson 4

Exercise 2 · Sort It: / ŭ / for o

▸ Listen to your teacher read the words in the **Word Bank** below.

Word Bank

done	none	front	son	some	one	ton	love
month	won	come	shove	dove	glove	once	from

▸ Group words that have the same phonogram (**done, none**) in each column.

▸ Put words that don't have the same phonogram as others (**front**) in the **Other** column.

-one	-ome	-ove	-on	Other

1. Do **none** and **won** rhyme? Why or why not?

   _____

   _____

2. Find other rhyming words in the **Word Bank**.

   _____

   _____

   _____

Exercise 3 · Find It: Possessives

▸ Find and underline the possessive word.

▸ Draw an arrow to the noun it refers to.

1. Max's best quiz

2. Lin-Yan's best sketches

3. Pam's bran muffins

4. Chan's socks

5. the notch on Beth's belt

6. the cut on Malik's chin

7. Frank's fish in the tank

8. my boss's stuck truck

9. Chad Smith's wishes for a van

10. many of Hank's saplings by the pond

Unit 9 · Lesson 4

Exercise 4 · Choose It and Use It

▸ Read the story below.

▸ Choose the best word for each blank from the **Word Bank**.

▸ Write the word in the blank.

Note: Some words can apply in more than one blank, but each word fits best into only one of the blanks.

Word Bank

pulling	bugs	ditches	buzzing	Brad's
puffing	scratches	branches	bull's	bulls

_____ bulls are huffing and _____.

They are _____ logs out of the _____.

The _____ get bad _____ from some of

the _____. Bugs are _____ around the

bulls. The _____ back is full of bugs. Brad yells at the

_____ to go away.

Exercise 5 · Rewrite It: Present Progressive to Past Progressive

▶ Read each sentence and circle the present progressive verb phrase.

▶ Rewrite each sentence, changing present progressive form to past progressive form.

▶ The first sentence is done as an example.

1. The vet's helper (is brushing) the dogs.

   The vet's helper was brushing the dogs.

2. Sam is passing math.

3. Mom and Alex are cutting these plums for the salad.

4. The truck is dumping trash in the landfill.

5. We are trusting her to welcome the incoming class.

Exercise 6 · Blueprint for Reading: Main Ideas and Transition Words

▸ Highlight the main ideas in blue.

▸ Circle the transition words: **one type**, **another type**, **the next type**, and **the final type**.

"How Bugs Bug Us"

You've heard this saying: "I've got a bug." You know what it means: "I'm sick." You can't see them, but bugs live all over your body. In fact, you're just a mini-zoo for bugs!

Bugs in Your Bed?

Dust mites are one type of bug on your body. Do you wash your pillow? No? If you use the same pillow every night for 10 years, half its weight is from dust mites. You can't see these tiny creatures. Still they are there, feeding on dead skin and sweat. Their droppings cause allergies. They make lots of us sick. Do your eyes sometimes get red and itchy? Does it happen when you shake out the spread on your bed? Does it happen when you sweep the floor? Then you're a victim of dust mites!

(continued)

Exercise 6 (continued) · Blueprint for Reading: Main Ideas and Transition Words

Stomach Alert!

Another type of bug that lives on your body is bacteria. Bacteria cover your body, inside and outside. No, you can't see them. They're too small. Most bacteria are not too bad, and some are even good. Bacteria help you digest food. Some bad bacteria are called germs. If you don't keep germs in check, they can spread. Germs can cause infection and make you sick.

In Your Hair?

The next type of bug that can live on your body is lice. Hair lice just love nice, clean hair. There, they can hunker down and guzzle blood from the scalp. They lay eggs on hair. Lice spread quickly! They spread from head to head. They spread when we work together closely, in school classrooms and at work. If we get lice, special shampoo can get rid of them.

Eyelash Horrors!

Eyelash mites are the final type of bug that exists on our body. You have mites in your eyelashes. Don't worry; they're harmless. These tiny bugs cling to eyelashes with eight tiny legs. They live on sebum, a natural oil in skin and hair. The truth is, lots of bugs just love our skin and hair!

Exercise 1 · Say and Write

▸ Say the sound your teacher says.

▸ Write the letter or letters for each sound.

1. _____   2. _____   3. _____   4. _____   5. _____

6. _____   7. _____   8. _____   9. _____   10. _____

Exercise 2 · Sort It: Vowel Sounds

▸ Label the columns with your teacher.

▸ Sort the words in the **Word Bank** according to their vowel sound / ŭ / or / ǒo / and spelling for / ŭ / (**u** or **o**).

▸ Write the word under the correct heading.

Word Bank

front	put	cut	push
rush	shove	from	bug
bush	done	pull	scrub

u = / ŭ /	**u** = / ǒo /	**o** = / ŭ /

1. Do **cut** and **put** rhyme? Why or why not?

_____

_____

2. Find the rhyming pair in the **Word Bank**.

_____

_____

Exercise 1 · Spelling Pretest 2

▸ Write the words your teacher says.

1. _____   6. _____   11. _____

2. _____   7. _____   12. _____

3. _____   8. _____   13. _____

4. _____   9. _____   14. _____

5. _____   10. _____   15. _____

Exercise 2 · Sort It: Word Meanings

▸ Read the words in the **Word Bank**.

▸ Sort the words into categories: **birds, mammals, containers, things to eat**.

Word Bank

puffin	cub	gull
bun	plum	nut
trunk	dog	jug
nutmeg	dove	chipmunk
mug	skunk	cup

Birds	Mammals	Containers	Things to Eat

Unit 9 · Lesson 6

Exercise 3 · Combine It: Direct Objects

▸ Read each sentence pair.

▸ Underline the direct object in both sentences.

▸ Write a compound direct object sentence on the line.

▸ Circle the conjunction **and** that joins the two direct objects.

▸ The first one is done as an example.

1. Jan had some <u>plums</u>. Jan had some <u>nuts</u>.

   Jan had some plums (and) nuts.

2. He swept the rug. He swept the steps.

   _____

3. They gave us junk. They gave us trash.

   _____

4. I cut some stems from the bush. I cut some buds from the bush.

   _____

5. He has a sax. He has a set of drums.

   _____

6. The path had many bumps. The path had many rocks.

   _____

7. She is fixing the rug. She is fixing the bed.

   _____

(continued)

Exercise 3 *(continued)* · **Combine It: Direct Objects**

8. They discussed their class. They discussed their prom.

_____

9. We have a bulldog. We have a Lab.

_____

10. I love sunsets. I love sunrises.

_____

Unit 9 · Lesson 6

▸ Use the penciling strategy to "scoop" the phrases in each sentence.

▸ Read the phrases as you would speak them.

▸ The first two are done for you.

1. Some bugs live in the grass.

2. A chinch bug is a pest.

3. This pest is bad for grass.

4. Bugs live on bushes and crops, too.

5. Bugs attack crops and kill them.

6. Getting rid of bugs is a big job.

7. You have to find where they live.

8. They are often hidden from us.

9. You can give them something toxic.

10. The toxins will kill them.

Exercise 5 · Find It: Words With / ŭ /

▸ Read the text quietly to yourself.

▸ Highlight all one-syllable words with / ŭ /.

▸ List five of the / ŭ / words on the lines below.

---

based on "Bad Bugs"

During hot months, chinch bugs lay eggs in the sod. The eggs hatch. Many of the small bugs live. These bugs kill grass. How? They attack grass stems. Then they suck on them. The grass wilts. This kills the grass.

Bugs live on bushes and crops, too. They can kill them. How? Bugs love to chomp on the plants' buds and stems.

---

1. _____

2. _____

3. _____

4. _____

5. _____

Exercise 1 · Contract It

▸ Read each contraction.

▸ Draw a line to the two words that make the contraction.

1. I'd		he would
2. it'd		we would
3. she'd		you would
4. he'd		I would
5. they'd		it would
6. we'd		she would
7. you'd		they would

▸ Read each contraction in the table below.

▸ Cross out the letters that get "squeezed out" or contracted.

▸ Replace them with an apostrophe (').

▸ Rewrite the contraction.

Read it	Cross out and replace	Rewrite it
1. I'd	I would	
2. it'd	it would	
3. she'd	she would	
4. he'd	he would	
5. they'd	they would	
6. we'd	we would	
7. you'd	you would	

Exercise 2 · Choose It and Use It: Singular or Plural

▸ Read each sentence.

▸ Choose and circle the singular or plural noun to fit the sentence.

▸ Copy the word you circled into the blank.

▸ Use the word that you copied in a sentence of your own.

1. Bud had many _____ on his legs from the bushes.

scratch or scratches

_____

2. Ann had a _____ of Patrick and the duck at the pond.

sketches or sketch

_____

3. Bud got six paint _____ from the shed.

brush or brushes

_____

4. The chimp hid in one of the _____ in the back of the pickup truck.

boxes or box

_____

5. Jill packs a _____ for the picnic.

lunch or lunches

_____

Unit 9 · Lesson 7

▸ Read the word in bold.

▸ Read the sentence.

▸ Add **-s**, **-es**, or **'s** to the word to write the correct form to fit the sentence.

▸ Write the word in the blank.

▸ Read your completed sentence to check that it sounds correct.

1. **rock**

   The fullback chucked ten _____ into the mud.

2. **batch**

   Mom picked up ten _____ of shrimp.

3. **Chuck**

   _____ pet bulldog can catch bugs.

4. **sketch**

   Jill _____ a duck on the pond at sunset.

5. **Frank**

   _____ snack shop has chops and clams for lunch.

6. **bug**

   Disgusting bed _____ chomped on his leg.

7. **nap**

   Juan _____ after lunch.

(continued)

8. snatch

The rapid rabbit _____ a snack every morning.

9. bunch

The chimps ate _____ of bananas.

10. Janet

We left _____ hat on the bench.

▸ Using words from these sentences:

- Write an example of a plural noun: _____

- Write an example of a possessive noun: _____

- Write an example of a third person singular, present tense verb: _____

Exercise 4 · Expand It: Direct Objects

▸ Read each sentence.

▸ Underline the direct object of the sentence.

▸ Create a second direct object for the sentence.

▸ Write your expanded sentence on the line.

▸ Underline the compound direct object.

▸ The first one is done as an example.

1. I could have a <u>drumstick</u>.

   I could have a <u>drumstick and a wing</u>.

2. We did chin-ups.

   _____

3. In math, I understand sets.

   _____

4. We had bunk beds.

   _____

5. She had a bucket.

   _____

6. Some bugs help plants.

   _____

7. They could track mud on the back steps.

   _____

(continued)

Exercise 4 (continued) · Expand It: Direct Objects

8. She welcomed the public, too.

_____

9. Dad is getting a pickup.

_____

10. They were pushing the desk across the classroom.

_____

Exercise 5 · Combine It: Direct Objects

▶ Combine these sentences using the conjunction **and**. Circle both direct objects.

1. Bed bugs invade blankets. Bed bugs invade mattresses.

_____

2. We fluff blankets. We fluff pillows.

_____

3. Some bugs eat plants. Some bugs eat flowers.

_____

4. Bed bugs eat dead skin. Bed bugs eat sweat.

_____

5. Bugs attack grass. Bugs attack crops.

_____

Lesson 8

Exercise 1 · Syllable Awareness: Segmentation

▸ Listen to and repeat the word your teacher says.

▸ Count the syllables in the word.

▸ Write the **letter** for each vowel sound you hear.

▸ Add the correct diacritical mark (breve) over the vowel letters to signal the short vowel sounds.

	How many syllables do you hear?	First Vowel Sound	Second Vowel Sound	Third Vowel Sound
1.				
2.				
3.				
4.				
5.				
6.				
7.				
8.				
9.				
10.				

Exercise 2 · Listening for Word Parts

▸ Listen to each word your teacher says.

▸ Write the part that your teacher repeats.

1. _____   2. _____   3. _____   4. _____   5. _____

6. _____   7. _____   8. _____   9. _____   10. _____

Exercise 3 · Sort It: Vowel Sounds

▸ Sort the word parts from Exercise 2, **Listening for Word Parts**, according to their vowel sound.

▸ Write the word parts with the same vowel sound in each column.

▸ After sorting, label the columns.

Unit 9 · Lesson 8

Exercise 4 · Word Networks: Antonyms, Synonyms, and Attributes

▶ Listen to each pair of words.

▶ Put an X in the column to show the relationship.

Word pair	Antonym	Synonym	Attribute
1. son: daughter			
2. cut: trim			
3. grapes: bunch			
4. luck: fortune			
5. income: money			
6. plus: minus			
7. animal: cub			
8. nothing: something			
9. tree: plum			
10. truck: dump			

Exercise 5 · Diagram It: Compound Direct Objects

▸ Diagram the first sentence with your teacher.

▸ Diagram the remaining sentences.

▸ Put an X over the vertical line that separates the subject from the predicate.

1. A bug's body often has three segments and six legs.

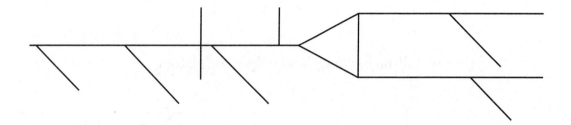

2. Some bugs quickly attack the plants and crops.

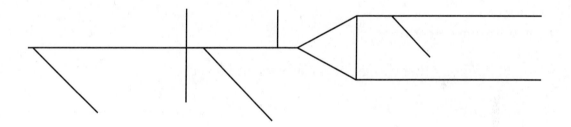

3. Chinch bugs sometimes kill the grass and the bushes.

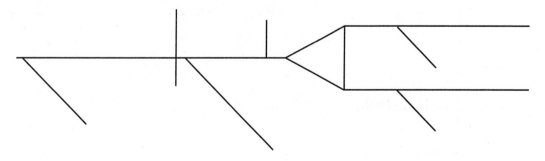

(continued)

Unit 9 · Lesson 8

4. In the hot months, chinch bugs transmit sickness and disease.

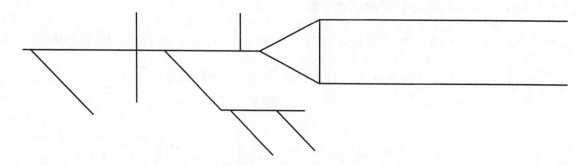

5. Toxins are killing bad bugs and helpful bugs, too.

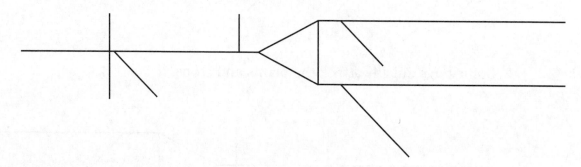

6. Among other things, bats eat bugs and insects.

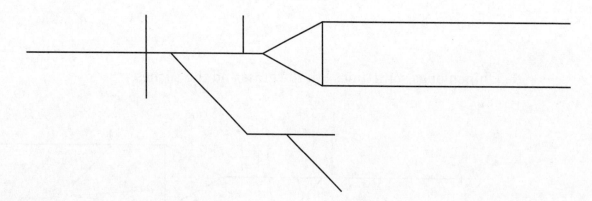

7. Bats and bugs help us and farmers, too.

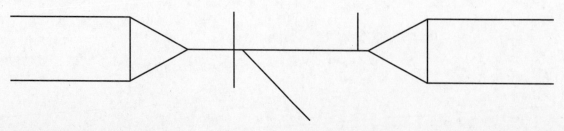

Exercise 5 (continued) · **Diagram It: Compound Direct Objects**

8. Sometimes, we upset nature's plans and balances.

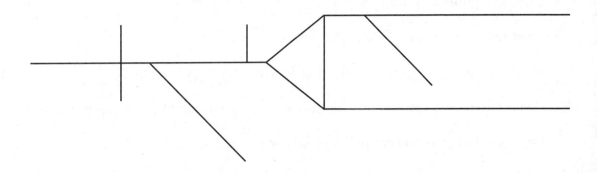

9. Once, nature governed plants and animals.

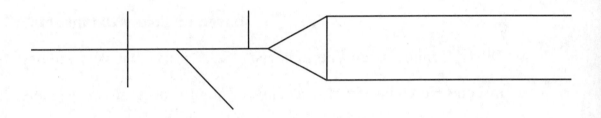

10. In our times, nature is losing plants and animals to toxins.

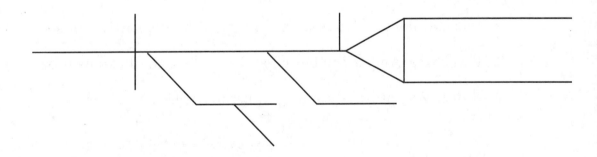

Exercise 6 · Use the Clues

▸ Use context clues to define the word **entomologist**.

▸ Underline the vocabulary word.

▸ Read the text surrounding the unknown word.

▸ Identify and circle the pronoun that follows the target word.

▸ Draw an arrow to show the link between the pronoun and the noun it refers to.

▸ Underline the words that help define the unknown word.

▸ Write a definition based on the context clues.

▸ Verify your definition with the dictionary or www.yourdictionary.com.

---

based on "New Old Insects"

Oliver Zompro is an entomologist. He is a scientist who studies insects. He comes from Germany. Zompro loves insects. People send him chunks of amber. Why do they send him amber? Amber is full of ancient insects. Amber is a rare stone that comes from ancient resin. Resin is a gum that drips from trees and covers insects. Millions of years pass. The resin hardens. It becomes as hard as stone. Amber can be yellow. It can be gold. It can be brown. Why does Zompro study amber? It is full of insect fossils.

---

entomologist- _____

_____

Exercise 7 · Answer It

▸ Answer each question in a complete sentence. Be sure to use part of the question in your answer.

1. Who is Oliver Zompro?

_____

_____

2. What did he discover in the chunk of amber?

_____

_____

3. When was a new order of insects found?

_____

_____

4. Where was the discovery made?

_____

_____

5. Tell why you think this discovery was important.

_____

_____

_____

_____

_____

Exercise 1 · Listening for Sounds in Words

▶ Write the letter that represents the vowel sound you hear in each word.

1. _____   2. _____   3. _____   4. _____   5. _____

6. _____   7. _____   8. _____   9. _____   10. _____

Exercise 2 · Syllable Awareness: Segmentation

▶ Listen to the word your teacher says.

▶ Count the syllables in the word.

▶ Write the letter for each vowel sound you hear.

	How many syllables do you hear?	First Vowel Sound	Second Vowel Sound	Third Vowel Sound
1.				
2.				
3.				
4.				
5.				
6.				
7.				
8.				
9.				
10.				

Exercise 3 · Sentence Dictation

▶ Listen to each sentence.

▶ Repeat the sentence.

▶ Write it on the line.

1. _____

2. _____

3. _____

4. _____

5. _____

▶ Read sentences 1, 2, and 3.

▶ Find the words that follow the **1 - 1 - 1** rule.

▶ Write them on the line.

_____

▶ Rewrite sentences 4 and 5. Replace the contraction with the expanded form.

_____

_____

Unit 9 · Lesson 9

Exercise 4 · Find It: Plural Noun Endings

▸ Read the following selection.

▸ Underline the nouns ending with **-s** or **-es**. (You should find 18.)

Camping With Bugs

Bud and Rosa had to cross some gulches to get to the cabin on the bluff. As they walked, the branches of some of the bushes stuck to Rosa's dress and scratched Bud's legs. They sat on one of the benches past the gulch to eat their lunch. A big, black, disgusting insect with a lot of fuzz landed on Bud's muffin. Rosa snatched the bug and flung it into one of the shrubs next to the path.

When they got to the rustic cabin, it was dusk. Big bugs buzzed on the front steps. The cabin was a dump, full of black dust and junk. A bad stench clung to the bunks and put Bud and Rosa into a funk. On top of that, Bud had left all of his matches back at the inn. Now what?

Rosa plucked lumps of disgusting fuzz from her bunk. Bud grunted that he had crushed six bed bugs. He said that he and Rosa would get bad rashes if they slept in the bunks. They ended up putting their mats down next to the bunks. When they got back, they were glad to have baths. Camping at the cabin with bugs had not been fun.

(continued)

Exercise 4 (continued) · Find It: Plural Noun Endings

▸ Answer these questions.

1. Explain why **-es** is used to form the plural with some nouns.

   _____

   _____

   _____

2. What two plural nouns are used as subjects?

   _____

   _____

3. Which five plural nouns have / ŭ /?

   _____

   _____

Exercise 5 · Information: Fact or Opinion?

▸ Listen to your teacher read **"New Old Insects."**

▸ Listen for information that gives facts or opinions about insects.

▸ List at least five facts and five opinions about studying insects in the spaces below.

FACTS about studying insects	OPINIONS about studying insects
Some examples: Oliver Zompro loves insects. New insects were found.	**Some examples:**
There can be many species in one order.	Some insects are odd.
There are many orders.	The entomologists hit pay dirt.
Entomologists are scientists who study insects.	The scientists were stunned.
Insect fossils can be found in chunks of amber.	Finding a new order of insects was big news.
Gladiators were the first new order of insects found in 87 years.	It was fantastic!

Exercise 6 · Take Note

Note-taking Guide	
Topic (**What was the article or program about?**)	_____ _____
Who or what?	_____ _____
What happened?	_____ _____ _____
When?	_____
Where?	_____ _____
Outcome or impact?	_____ _____
Why important?	_____ _____ _____ _____

(continued)

Unit 9 · Lesson 9

Summary

_____

_____

_____

_____

_____

_____

_____

_____

Exercise 1 · Listening for Sounds in Words

▸ Listen to your teacher say each word.

▸ Write the letter or letters for the sounds you hear in each word in the boxes.

▸ Circle the words with **o** for / ŭ /.

▸ Put a box around the words with **u** for / oͦo /.

1.

2.

3.

4.

5.

6.

7.

8.

9.

10.

Unit 9 · Lesson 10

Exercise 2 · Sort It: Word Meanings

▸ Listen and follow along as your teacher rereads the last paragraph of **"New Old Insects"** below.

▸ Listen for words that name **kinds of insects** and **parts of insects**.

▸ Underline them in the text below when you hear them.

▸ Sort the words into the table categories.

from "New Old Insects"

The new order of insects is called *mantophasmatodea* (pronounced 'măn-tə 'făz-mə 'tō-dē-ə). These insects have a nickname: Gladiators. They look like other insects, such as the walking stick or the praying mantis. But they are predators. They have long antennae, sharp jaws, and three small teeth. Until this time, they were unknown. There had been no books on these insects. Now they are recorded! They are a new order! They are new old insects!

Kinds of insects	Parts of insects

Exercise 3 · Define It

▸ Listen and follow along as your teacher reads the text below.

▸ Sort the underlined words into the "Category" or "Attributes" column.

▸ Use the text to define the word **mantophasmatodea**.

▸ Use the category and attributes words to write a definition.

---

based on "New Old Insects"

The new order of insects is called *mantophasmatodea*. These insects have a nickname: Gladiators. They look like a praying mantis. They are predators. They have long antennae, sharp jaws, and three small teeth.

Mantophasmatodea:

Category	Attributes

Mantophasmatodea _____

_____

_____

Lesson Checklist
Lessons 1–2

Check off the activities you complete with each lesson. Evaluate your accomplishments at the end of each lesson. Pay attention to teacher evaluations and comments.

Unit Objectives	Lesson 1 (Date:_____)	Lesson 2 (Date:_____)
STEP 1 **Phonemic Awareness and Phonics** • Say the long vowel sound for each vowel <u>a</u>, <u>e</u>, <u>i</u>, <u>o</u>, <u>u</u>. • Write the letter pattern to represent the long vowel sound a_e, e_e, i_e, o_e, u_e. • Identify syllables in spoken words.	❑ Move It and Mark it ❑ Phonemic Drills ❑ Listening for Sounds in Words ❑ Handwriting Practice	❑ Using the Vowel Chart (T) ❑ Phonemic Drills ❑ See and Say ❑ Say and Write
STEP 2 **Word Recognition and Spelling** • Read and spell words with sound-spelling correspondences from this and previous units. • Read and spell the **Essential Words:** *although, almost, already, always, also, alone.* • Read and spell contractions with **will**.	❑ Exercise 1: Spelling Pretest 1 ❑ Build It ❑ Memorize It	❑ Build It, Bank It ❑ Word Fluency 1 ❑ Memorize It ❑ Handwriting Practice
STEP 3 **Vocabulary and Morphology** • Define **Unit Vocabulary** words. • Identify and generate synonyms, antonyms, and homophones for **Unit Vocabulary**. • Add **-s** to verbs to signal third person singular, present tense; **-ed** to signal past tense; and **-ing** to signal present progressive.	❑ Unit Vocabulary ❑ Multiple Meaning Map ❑ Exercise 2: Word Relationships: Homophones ❑ Expression of the Day	❑ Exercise 1: Find It: Present Tense Verb Endings ❑ Exercise 2: Add It ❑ Expression of the Day
STEP 4 **Grammar and Usage** • Identify future tense verb phrases. • Identify compound sentences.	❑ Exercise 3: Rewrite It: Proper and Common Nouns ❑ Exercise 4: Identify It: Concrete and Abstract Nouns	❑ Exercise 3: Identify It: Irregular Verb Forms
STEP 5 **Listening and Reading Comprehension** • Read fluently with inflection, phrasing, and expression. • Identify time sequence organization in informational text. • Select context clues from informational text.	❑ Exercise 5: Phrase It ❑ Decodable Text: "Past Time" ❑ Exercise 6: Find It: Words With Final Silent <u>e</u>	❑ Passage Fluency 1
STEP 6 **Speaking and Writing** • Generate sentences that present facts. • Write a time sequence paragraph using transition words. • Answer **Understand It** questions beginning with **paraphrase, summarize,** and **identify**. • Record information on a graphic organizer.	❑ Masterpiece Sentences: Stages 1–3	❑ Exercise 4: Combine It: Compound Sentence Parts
Self-Evaluation (5 is the highest) **Effort** = I produced my best work. **Participation** = I was actively involved in tasks. **Independence** = I worked on my own.	Effort: 1 2 3 4 5 Participation: 1 2 3 4 5 Independence: 1 2 3 4 5	Effort: 1 2 3 4 5 Participation: 1 2 3 4 5 Independence: 1 2 3 4 5
Teacher Evaluation	Effort: 1 2 3 4 5 Participation: 1 2 3 4 5 Independence: 1 2 3 4 5	Effort: 1 2 3 4 5 Participation: 1 2 3 4 5 Independence: 1 2 3 4 5

Lesson 3 (Date:_____)	**Lesson 4** (Date:_____)	**Lesson 5** (Date:_____)
❑ Vowel + Consonant + **e** Pattern ❑ Phonemic Drills ❑ Listening for Sounds in Words	❑ Phonemic Drills ❑ Exercise 1: Listening for Sounds in Words ❑ Letter-Sound Fluency	❑ Phonemic Drills ❑ Letter-Sound Fluency ❑ Exercise 1: Say and Write ❑ Content Mastery: Sound-Spelling Correspondences
❑ Exercise 1: Listening for Word Parts ❑ Word Fluency 1 ❑ Exercise 2: Find It: Essential Words	❑ Drop **e** Rule ❑ Drop It (T) ❑ Word Fluency 2 ❑ Type It: Essential Words ❑ Handwriting Practice	❑ Content Mastery: Spelling Posttest 1 ❑ Exercise 2: Sort It: Words Ending in **v**
❑ Exercise 3: Word Networks: Antonyms ❑ Draw It: Idioms ❑ Expression of the Day	❑ Exercise 2: Find It: Present and Present Progressive ❑ Expression of the Day	❑ Multiple Meaning Map (T) ❑ Expression of the Day
❑ Exercise 4: Find It: Verb Phrases ❑ Exercise 5: Rewrite It: Future Tense ❑ Exercise 6: Identify It: Past, Present, or Future	❑ Exercise 3: Sort It: Verb Tenses	❑ Masterpiece Sentences: Stages 1–6 ❑ Using Masterpiece Sentences: Changing the Verb to Future Tense
❑ Exercise 7: Use the Clues	❑ Exercise 4: Blueprint For Reading: Time Sequence	❑ Exercise 4: Blueprint for Reading: Time Sequence (Lesson 4)
❑ Exercise 8: Answer It	❑ Exercise 5: Blueprint for Writing: Outline (T) ❑ Challenge Text: "Creating the Calendar"	❑ Blueprint for Writing: Outline (T) ❑ Write It: Time Sequence Paragraph ❑ Challenge Text: "Creating the Calendar"
Effort: 1 2 3 4 5 **Participation:** 1 2 3 4 5 **Independence:** 1 2 3 4 5	**Effort:** 1 2 3 4 5 **Participation:** 1 2 3 4 5 **Independence:** 1 2 3 4 5	**Effort:** 1 2 3 4 5 **Participation:** 1 2 3 4 5 **Independence:** 1 2 3 4 5
Effort: 1 2 3 4 5 **Participation:** 1 2 3 4 5 **Independence:** 1 2 3 4 5	**Effort:** 1 2 3 4 5 **Participation:** 1 2 3 4 5 **Independence:** 1 2 3 4 5	**Effort:** 1 2 3 4 5 **Participation:** 1 2 3 4 5 **Independence:** 1 2 3 4 5

Check off the activities you complete with each lesson. Evaluate your accomplishments at the end of each lesson. Pay attention to teacher evaluations and comments.

	Unit Objectives	Lesson 6 (Date:_____)	Lesson 7 (Date:_____)
STEP 1	**Phonemic Awareness and Phonics** • Say the long vowel sound for each vowel <u>a</u>, <u>e</u>, <u>i</u>, <u>o</u>, <u>u</u>. • Write the letter pattern to represent the long vowel sound a_e, e_e, i_e, o_e, u_e. • Identify syllables in spoken words.	❑ Phonemic Drills ❑ Exercise 1: Listening for Sounds in Words ❑ Handwriting Practice	❑ Phonemic Drills ❑ See and Name ❑ Name and Write ❑ Listening for Sounds In Words ❑ Syllable Awareness: Segmentation
STEP 2	**Word Recognition and Spelling** • Read and spell words with sound-spelling correspondences from this and previous units. • Read and spell the **Essential Words:** *although, almost, already, always, also, alone.* • Read and spell contractions with **will**.	❑ Exercise 2: Spelling Pretest 2 ❑ Exercise 3: Listening for Word Parts ❑ Word Fluency 3	❑ Exercise 1: Contract It ❑ Drop It: Drop <u>e</u> Rule (T)
STEP 3	**Vocabulary and Morphology** • Define **Unit Vocabulary** words. • Identify and generate synonyms, antonyms, and homophones for **Unit Vocabulary**. • Add **-s** to verbs to signal third person singular, present tense; **-ed** to signal past tense; and **-ing** to signal present progressive.	❑ Unit Vocabulary ❑ Exercise 4: Sort It: Meaning Categories (T) ❑ Expression of the Day	❑ Exercise 2: Rewrite It: Present Progressive to Past ❑ Exercise 3: Identify It: Verb Forms ❑ Expression of the Day
STEP 4	**Grammar and Usage** • Identify future tense verb phrases. • Identify compound sentences.	❑ Exercise 5: Identify It and Diagram It	❑ Compound Sentences ❑ Exercise 4: Combine It: Compound Sentences
STEP 5	**Listening and Reading Comprehension** • Identify time sequence organization in informational text. • Select context clues from informational text.	❑ Exercise 6: Phrase It ❑ Decodable Text: "It's About Time" ❑ Exercise 7: Find It: Words With Final Silent <u>e</u>	❑ Passage Fluency 2
STEP 6	**Speaking and Writing** • Generate sentences that present facts. • Write a time sequence paragraph using transition words. • Answer **Understand It** questions beginning with **paraphrase, summarize,** and **identify**.	❑ Masterpiece Sentences: Compound Sentence Parts	❑ Exercise 5: Combine It: More Compound Sentences
	Self-Evaluation (5 is the highest) **Effort** = I produced my best work. **Participation** = I was actively involved in tasks. **Independence** = I worked on my own.	**Effort:** 1 2 3 4 5 **Participation:** 1 2 3 4 5 **Independence:** 1 2 3 4 5	**Effort:** 1 2 3 4 5 **Participation:** 1 2 3 4 5 **Independence:** 1 2 3 4 5
	Teacher Evaluation	**Effort:** 1 2 3 4 5 **Participation:** 1 2 3 4 5 **Independence:** 1 2 3 4 5	**Effort:** 1 2 3 4 5 **Participation:** 1 2 3 4 5 **Independence:** 1 2 3 4 5

Lesson 8 (Date:_____)	**Lesson 9** (Date:_____)	**Lesson 10** (Date:_____)
❏ Phonemic Drills ❏ Letter-Name Fluency ❏ Exercise 1: Syllable Awareness: Segmentation	❏ Phonemic Drills ❏ Letter-Name Fluency ❏ Exercise 1: Listening for Sounds in Words ❏ Exercise 2: Syllable Awareness: Segmentation (T)	❏ Exercise 1: Listening for Sounds in Words
❏ Exercise 2: Sort It: Number of Syllables ❏ Word Fluency 4	❏ Exercise 3: Sentence Dictation ❏ Drop It: Drop **e** Rule (T)	❏ Content Mastery: Spelling Posttest 2
❏ Exercise 3: Word Relationships: Synonyms ❏ Content Mastery: Word Relationships	❏ Exercise 4: Find It: Verb Forms ❏ Exercise 5: Rewrite It: Verb Forms ❏ Expression of the Day	❏ Define It (T) ❏ Draw It: Idioms ❏ Expression of the Day
❏ Exercise 4: Diagram It: Compound Sentences (T)	❏ Masterpiece Sentences: Building Compound Sentences	❏ Content Mastery: Verb Tense; Compound Sentences
❏ Instructional Text: "Time Zones" ❏ Exercise 5: Use the Clues	❏ Exercise 6: Draw It: Listening for Information	❏ Listening for Information
❏ Exercise 6: Answer It	❏ Exercise 7: Answer It ❏ Challenge Text: "The Time Machine"	❏ Blueprint for Writing: Developing Main Ideas ❏ Challenge Text: "The Time Machine"
Effort: 1 2 3 4 5 **Participation:** 1 2 3 4 5 **Independence:** 1 2 3 4 5	**Effort:** 1 2 3 4 5 **Participation:** 1 2 3 4 5 **Independence:** 1 2 3 4 5	**Effort:** 1 2 3 4 5 **Participation:** 1 2 3 4 5 **Independence:** 1 2 3 4 5
Effort: 1 2 3 4 5 **Participation:** 1 2 3 4 5 **Independence:** 1 2 3 4 5	**Effort:** 1 2 3 4 5 **Participation:** 1 2 3 4 5 **Independence:** 1 2 3 4 5	**Effort:** 1 2 3 4 5 **Participation:** 1 2 3 4 5 **Independence:** 1 2 3 4 5

Exercise 1 · Spelling Pretest 1

▸ Write each word your teacher repeats.

1. _____   6. _____   11. _____

2. _____   7. _____   12. _____

3. _____   8. _____   13. _____

4. _____   9. _____   14. _____

5. _____   10. _____   15. _____

Exercise 2 · Word Relationships: Homophones

▶ Write the words **passed** and **past** on the lines in the Venn diagram.

▶ Fill in information about both words.

▶ Identify what is the same about the two words.

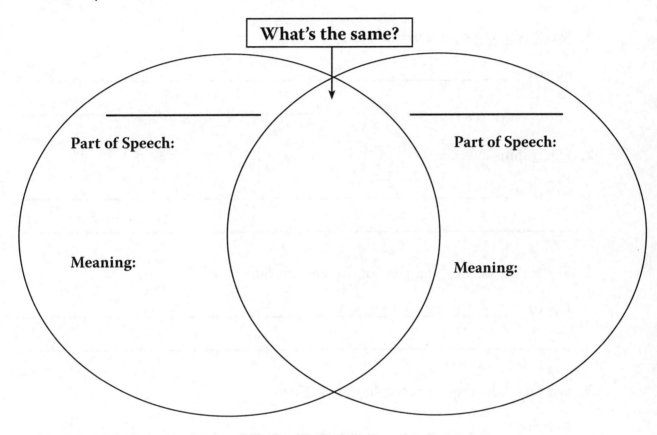

What's the same?

_____   _____

Part of Speech: Part of Speech:

Meaning: Meaning:

▶ Fill in the following blanks with **passed** or **past**.
   Hint: If the missing word is a verb, it is spelled **passed**.

1. Time _____ us by.

2. Home videos help us remember the _____ .

3. The sentence has a _____ tense verb.

4. I _____ my driver's test.

5. The test ran _____ lunchtime.

Unit 10 · Lesson 1

Exercise 3 · Rewrite It: Proper and Common Nouns

▸ Read the sentence, and note the underlined proper noun.

▸ Rewrite the sentence, changing the underlined proper noun to a common noun.

▸ Circle the common noun in your new sentence.

1. <u>Mt. Rushmore</u> stands in the mist.

   Rewrite: _____

   _____

2. <u>Earth</u> spins in space.

   Rewrite: _____

   _____

3. The time zone in <u>Atlanta</u> is not the same as ours.

   Rewrite: _____

   _____

4. On their trip, they went to <u>Mammoth Cave</u>.

   Rewrite: _____

   _____

5. <u>Mr. Moto</u> collects grandfather clocks.

   Rewrite: _____

   _____

6. The <u>Egyptians</u> had no clock, but they could track the passing of time.

   Rewrite: _____

   _____

(continued)

7. The <u>Greeks</u> used sand to track the passing of time.

   Rewrite: _____

   _____

8. By the late 1200s, <u>London</u> had clocks that chimed and rang.

   Rewrite: _____

   _____

9. In 1577, <u>Jost Burgi</u> invented the minute hand.

   Rewrite: _____

   _____

10. With string, <u>Pascal</u> attached his pocket watch to his wrist.

    Rewrite: _____

    _____

Exercise 4: Identify It: Concrete and Abstract Nouns

▸ Listen to your teacher read each sentence.

▸ Identify the underlined noun as **concrete** or **abstract**.

▸ Write C (*concrete*) or A (*abstract*) in the blank.

▸ The first one is done for you.

1. Mt. Rushmore stands in the <u>mist</u>.
   (*Mist* can be felt; it is not an *idea*; it is concrete.)   _____C_____

2. The planet spins in <u>space</u>.   _____

3. The city's time <u>zone</u> is not the same as ours.   _____

4. On their <u>trip</u>, they went to Mammoth Cave.   _____

5. Mr. Moto collects grandfather <u>clocks</u>.   _____

6. Egyptians had no clock, but they could track
   the passing of <u>time</u>.   _____

7. The Greeks had used <u>sand</u> to track the
   passing of time.   _____

8. By the late <u>1200s</u>, London had clocks that
   chimed and rang.   _____

9. In 1577, Jost Burgi invented the minute <u>hand</u>.   _____

10. Pascal attached his pocket watch to his
    <u>wrist</u> with string.   _____

Exercise 5 · Phrase It

▸ Use the penciling strategy to "scoop" the phrases in each sentence.

▸ Read as you would speak them.

▸ The first two are done for you.

Time is passing.

We track time as our planet moves.

Think of the past.

People made things to track time.

A sundial let people tell time.

It tracked the sun's shade.

They could guess the time for sunrise

An hourglass was not like these things.

It had sand inside.

The sand let people track time.

Unit 10 · Lesson 1

Exercise 6 · Find It: Words With Final Silent e

▸ Highlight or underline the one-syllable words with a **final silent e**.

▸ Record five different **final silent e** words on the lines below.

based on "Past Time"

Men made sundials. A sundial let men tell time. It tracked the sun's shade. An object sat on the sundial's face. It cast the shade in an exact place. It let men guess the time. It was fine if the sun was out. If it was not, what did men do? They made thick, waxed strings. They made notches in the wax. At sunset, men lit them. They lit them at the top. They noted the time passing. The wax melted. The flame made the wax melt. Time passed. At what rate did it melt? They could guess the time for sunrise.

1. _____

2. _____

3. _____

4. _____

5. _____

Unit 10 · Lesson 2

Exercise 1 • Find It: Present Tense Verb Endings

Part 1

▸ Read the sentences and underline the present tense verb.

    1. My watch tells time.

    2. He hunts in the spring.

    3. Each morning, Steve plugs in the lamp.

    4. When the mule stops, Pete shakes his fist.

    5. The van stops when the light is red.

▸ Listen to your teacher read the words in the **Word Bank** and each sentence with a blank.

▸ Select the word to fill in the blanks to tell about the underlined verb.

Word Bank

suffix	one	singular	third	present

    1. The **-s** is a _____ added to these verbs.

    2. The verb is in the _____ person, which means that you are talking to someone about one or more other people or things.

    3. The verb is in the _____ tense, which means now.

    4. The verb agrees with _____ nouns or pronouns.

    5. Singular means just _____.

Part 2

▸ Read these sentences and underline the verb(s) in each.

    1. He faxes the note to his wife and watches for one from her.

(continued)

Exercise 1 (continued) · Find It: Present Tense Verb Endings

2. Carlos catches a fast ball.

3. Mike bosses his kid sister.

4. Jake punches the time clock when he starts work.

5. Jan chats on the phone with her dad.

▶ Listen to your teacher read the words in the **Word Bank** and each sentence with a blank.

▶ Select the word to fill in the blanks to tell about the underlined verb.

Word Bank

-es   singular   third   present   <u>ch</u>, -<u>tch</u>, <u>sh</u>, <u>s</u>, <u>x</u>, and <u>z</u>

1. These verbs use the suffix **-es** to show that they are _____ tense,

   _____ person _____ verbs.

2. We use **-es** to show the third person singular present tense verb after the

   letters: _____

3. The **e** in the suffix _____ helps us hear the suffix more clearly.

Part 3

▶ Read these sentences and underline the verb phrase in each.

1. Summertime is passing quickly.

2. The kids are snacking on grapes.

3. I am swinging into the sky.

4. Jake is backing the truck up to the shed.

5. All the clocks are chiming at the same time.

(continued)

Exercise 1 (continued) · Find It: Present Tense Verb Endings

▶ Listen to your teacher read the words in the **Word Bank** and each sentence with blanks.

▶ Select the word to fill in the blanks to tell about the underlined verb.

Word Bank

-ing	are	is	am	progressive

1. The verbs end with the suffix _____.

2. The verbs are in a phrase. The phrase is made up of the **-ing** form of the verb and _____, _____, or _____.

3. They all show the present _____, which means the action is ongoing in the present, or now.

Unit 10 · Lesson 2

Exercise 2 · Add It

▸ Read the sentence quietly to yourself.

▸ Decide if the verb needs -**s** or -**es**.

▸ Add the suffix to form a third person singular, present tense verb.

▸ Copy the word with the suffix.

Add the suffix -**s** or -**es**:	Copy the verb with the suffix:
Examples:	
June push**es**.	pushes
Mike honk **s** .	honks
The ape wade **s** .	wades
1. Jack brand___.	1. _____
2. The mule kick___.	2. _____
3. The pop fizz___.	3. _____
4. Jake send___ stamps.	4. _____
5. Jane press___ the tube.	5. _____

Exercise 3 · Identify It: Irregular Verb Forms

▸ Use the irregular past tense verbs in the chart in the *Student Text*, page 113.

▸ Read the present tense verbs in the chart below, and identify the past forms.

▸ Write the irregular past tense forms of the verbs in the **Past** column.
The last two are a review.

▸ The first one is done as an example.

	Present	Past
1.	dive	dove
2.	make	
3.	ride	
4.	rise	
5.	shake	
6.	shine	
7.	take	
8.	wake	
9.	write	
10.	give	

Exercise 4 · Combine It: Compound Sentence Parts

▸ Combine these sentences into one sentence using the conjunction **and**.

▸ Write the sentence on the line.

▸ Circle the part of the sentence that is compounded.

1. Our planet moves.
   Our planet spins.   subject / predicate / direct object

   _____

2. Men made sundials.
   Men made waxed strings.   subject / predicate / direct object

   _____

3. Sundials let men tell time.
   Sand lets men tell time.   subject / predicate / direct object

   _____

4. Sand moved from the top.
   Sand went into a hole.   subject / predicate / direct object

   _____

5. The hourglass was not exact.
   The sundial was not exact.   subject / predicate / direct object

   _____

Exercise 1 · Listening for Word Parts

▸ Listen to each word.

▸ Write each word part that your teacher repeats.

1. _____   2. _____   3. _____   4. _____   5. _____

6. _____   7. _____   8. _____   9. _____   10. _____

Unit 10 · Lesson 3

Exercise 2 · Find It: Essential Words

▸ Find the **Essential Words** for this unit in each sentence.

▸ Underline them.

1. It must be almost 100 degrees out.

2. That clock already tells the exact time.

3. The rafts have already drifted away.

4. Although he was sick many days, he still passed the math test.

5. It's almost time for the sun to set.

6. Time zones have always helped to set the exact time.

7. Although they didn't get the top prize, they did their best in the game.

8. Dale always goes to the shop with her.

9. Chung and Calvin also went to the game.

10. Juan worked alone in his shed until 9 o'clock.

11. Did you also go for a swim in the lake?

12. Were you alone when you fell?

13. She always gave the best gifts.

14. I was also with her when she fell off her bike.

15. I have gone alone to the bike shop many times.

▸ Write the **Essential Words** in the spaces.

_____ _____ _____ _____ _____ _____

Exercise 3 · Word Networks: Antonyms

▶ Read the words in the **Word Bank**.

Word Bank

hate	life	rise	same	take
hope	ride	safe	save	wide

▶ Write the antonym (opposite) for each word your teacher says.

1. fear   _____

2. death   _____

3. like   _____

4. walk   _____

5. fall   _____

6. dangerous   _____

7. different   _____

8. spend   _____

9. give   _____

10. narrow   _____

Exercise 4 · Find It: Verb Phrases

▶ Read the sentence.

▶ Find and underline the verb phrase.

▶ The first one is done for you.

1. She <u>is chatting</u> with him.

2. Joe is riding the bus.

3. We are asking for help.

4. He was making a sandwich.

5. They were diving into the lake.

Unit 10 · Lesson 3

Exercise 5 · Rewrite It: Future Tense

▸ Review the **Tense Timeline**.

▸ Rewrite each present tense verb as a future tense verb phrase.

▸ The first one is done for you.

Tense Timeline

Yesterday	Today	Tomorrow
Past	Present	Future
Example:	chase	will chase
1.	dive	_____
2.	fade	_____
3.	hike	_____
4.	hope	_____
5.	make	_____

Exercise 6 · Identify It: Past, Present, or Future

▸ Look at the underlined verb phrase in each sentence below.

▸ Circle the word in the phrase that signals past, present, or future.

▸ Put an X in the correct column to indicate past, present, or future tense for the verb phrase.

▸ The first one is done for you.

1. They (will) swim across the lake.

2. The cloth will fade in the sun.

3. The horses were running fast.

4. Fire trucks and ambulances are rushing through the streets.

5. Clocks were chiming at six o'clock.

6. I will arrive early.

7. They will tame the pets.

8. She is shaking the kite's rope.

9. They were naming the winners.

10. Our class will quote Shakespeare.

(continued)

Unit 10 · Lesson 3

	Past	Present	Future
1.			X
2.			
3.			
4.			
5.			
6.			
7.			
8.			
9.			
10.			

Exercise 7 · Use the Clues

▶ Use context clues and pronoun referents to define the phrase **Sung Dynasty**.

- Underline the vocabulary words.

- Read the text surrounding the unknown words.

- Identify and circle the pronouns that follow the unknown words.

- Draw an arrow to show the link between the pronoun and the noun it refers to.

- Underline the text that helps you learn about the words.

---

from "Telling Time"

Then, people burned candles to tell time. This happened around the year AD 1000. Two different civilizations had the same idea. Each was far from the other. But they began using the same method to tell time. Alfred the Great was a king. He was a Saxon king. He ruled in an area that is now part of England. The Saxons burned candles to tell time. The **Sung Dynasty** had power in China. They ruled about the same time period. They, too, burned candles to mark time.

▶ Write a definition based on the context clues.

▶ Verify your definition with the dictionary or www.yourdictionary.com.

Note: Answers will vary.

Definition:

Sung Dynasty: _____

_____

Unit 10 · Lesson 3

Exercise 8 · Answer It

- Underline the signal word.

- Answer each question in a complete sentence.

- Underline the part of the sentence that answers the question.

1. When did the Egyptians use the sundial?

   _____

   _____

2. When was water used to tell time?

   _____

   _____

3. Identify two civilizations that used candles to tell time.

   Two civilizations that used candles to tell time were the _____

   and the _____ .

4. Identify two parts in a mechanical clock.

   Two parts in a mechanical clock are a _____ and a

   _____ .

5. Identify the type of atom used in the most precise atomic clock.

   The _____ is used in the most precise atomic clock.

Exercise 1 · Listening for Sounds in Words

▸ Listen to each word the teacher says.

▸ Identify the vowel and decide if it is short or long.

▸ Say the sound as you write the letter or letters to represent the vowel.

1. _____   2. _____   3. _____   4. _____   5. _____

6. _____   7. _____   8. _____   9. _____   10. _____

Exercise 2 · Find It: Present and Present Progressive

▸ Read each sentence.

▸ Underline the present tense verbs.

▸ Circle the present progressive verbs.

> **Examples:**
>
> They <u>ask</u> the twins for a drink of milk.
>
> She (is fixing) her tent with duct tape.

1. That subject makes me mad.

2. The sun is rising later day by day.

3. The gull dives down to grab a bit of muffin.

4. The tree is shading the backyard.

5. Steve shoves the dust under the rug.

6. Jane fixes pickup trucks for fun.

7. Pat is ripping up the tiles next to the bathtub.

8. We are planning a visit to Steve's home state.

9. With a wide smile, the chimp swings from vine to vine.

10. Nick is rushing home with a pup for his brother.

Unit 10 · Lesson 4

Exercise 3 · Sort It: Verb Tenses

▸ Read the following sentences from **"It's About Time."**

▸ Find the underlined verbs and verb phrases in order of the numbers.

▸ Sort the verbs and verb phrases into past, present, and future tense.

▸ Write the verb or verb phrase in the correct column.

▸ The first one is done for you.

---

based on "It's About Time"

Where do you <u>live</u>? What time zone <u>is</u> it? The globe <u>has</u> 24 time zones.
       1   2   3

Time zone lines <u>were made</u> to run from pole to pole. As you go around the
              4

globe, you <u>cross</u> from zone to zone. You <u>adjust</u> your clock as you travel. You
         5   6

<u>will set</u> the time up or back an hour. What if you take a long drive? Drive
  7

west, and you <u>will set</u> your clock back. Drive east, and you <u>will lose</u> an hour.
          8   9

You <u>will adjust</u> your clock.
      10

What about long trips? <u>Think</u> about planes. Planes <u>will cross</u> many time
            11   12

zones. When a plane <u>left</u> Wisconsin, the time <u>was</u> 6:00 P.M. The plane
          13   14

<u>will cross</u> 12 time zones. When it lands, it <u>will be</u> 6:00 A.M. On the other
  15   16

side of the globe, it <u>will be</u> the next day! Your body's clock <u>tells</u> you one
         17   18

time. But the clock in this time zone <u>is</u> not the same. You <u>have</u> jet lag!
                 19   20

(continued)

Exercise 3 (continued) · Sort It: Verb Tenses

	Past	Present	Future
1.		live	
2.			
3.			
4.			
5.			
6.			
7.			
8.			
9.			
10.			
11.			
12.			
13.			
14.			
15.			
16.			
17.			
18.			
19.			
20.			

Exercise 4 · Blueprint for Reading: Time Sequence

▸ Highlight each method of telling time in blue.

▸ Circle the transition words or phrases.

---

from "Telling Time"

First the sundial was used to tell time. It was used from about 1500 to 1300 BC. The Egyptians measured the time of day. How? They measured the sun's shadow. Days were shorter during the winter. They were longer during the summer. The sun almost always shines in Egypt. This method was a good one for these early people.

Later, during the 1400s, the first mechanical clocks appeared. These were built in Europe. They used a mainspring and balance wheel. Now, telling time relied upon a mechanical device.

Finally, around 1950, we all began to use atomic clocks. Isador Rabi was the first one to think of this idea. He was a physicist. His clock was based on the study of atoms. Atomic clocks measure the vibration of atoms. By 1967, time became even more precise. One second was defined. It was 9,192,631,770 vibrations of the cesium atom. In 1993, the latest atomic clock came on line. It had even more incredible accuracy. Now everyone around the world measures time the same way.

Exercise 5 · Blueprint for Writing: Outline

Topic _____

First

Main
Idea

I. _____

A. _____

B. _____

C. _____

D. _____

Later

Main
Idea

II. _____

A. _____

B. _____

C. _____

D. _____

Finally

Main
Idea

III. _____

A. _____

B. _____

C. _____

D. _____

Conclusion _____

Exercise 1 · Say and Write

▸ Write the letter for each sound your teacher says.

▸ Say the sound as you write the letter.

1. _____ 2. _____ 3. _____ 4. _____ 5. _____

6. _____ 7. _____ 8. _____ 9. _____ 10. _____

Exercise 2 · Sort It: Words Ending in v

▸ Label the columns: **short, long**.

▸ Sort the words in the **Word Bank** by vowel sound.

▸ Write each word in the correct column. One of the words can be in both columns.

Word Bank

give	jive	gave	save	have
hive	wave	rave	dive	live

Short	Long

Exercise 1 · Listening for Sounds in Words

▸ Listen to each word the teacher says.

▸ Identify the vowel sound and decide if it is short or long.

▸ Circle the vowel with the correct diacritical mark.

Short = (˘)
Long = (¯)

	a	e	i	o	u	oo
1.	a	e	i	o	u	oo
2.	a	e	i	o	u	oo
3.	a	e	i	o	u	oo
4.	a	e	i	o	u	oo
5.	a	e	i	o	u	oo
6.	a	e	i	o	u	oo
7.	a	e	i	o	u	oo
8.	a	e	i	o	u	oo
9.	a	e	i	o	u	oo
10.	a	e	i	o	u	oo

Exercise 2 · Spelling Pretest 2

▸ Write each word your teacher repeats.

1. _____   6. _____   11. _____

2. _____   7. _____   12. _____

3. _____   8. _____   13. _____

4. _____   9. _____   14. _____

5. _____   10. _____   15. _____

Exercise 3 · Listening for Word Parts

▸ Listen to each word.

▸ Write each word part that your teacher repeats.

1. _____   2. _____   3. _____   4. _____   5. _____

6. _____   7. _____   8. _____   9. _____   10. _____

Exercise 4 · Sort It: Meaning Categories

▸ Read the words in the **Word Bank** and at the top of each column.

▸ Sort the words in the **Word Bank** into the three categories.

▸ Write the words in the correct column.

Hint: One word can be used in two columns.

Word Bank

slope	where	size
many	spring	when
inside	sunset	cave
bakeshop	nine	sunrise
home	five	eve

Number	Time	Place

Exercise 5 · Identify It and Diagram It

For each set of sentences:

▸ First, circle the conjunction **and**.

▸ Then, underline the two sentence parts that are compounded in the sentence.

▸ Next, diagram sentences 2 and 3.

▸ The first sentence is done for you in each set.

Compound Subject

  1. Time (and) tide wait for no man.

  2. The haze and fog lifted.

  3. London and Rome have many visitors.

  1. Time and tide wait for no man.

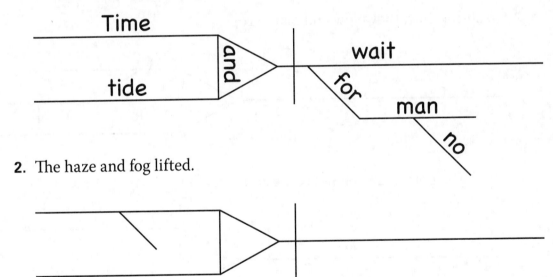

  2. The haze and fog lifted.

  3. London and Rome have many visitors.

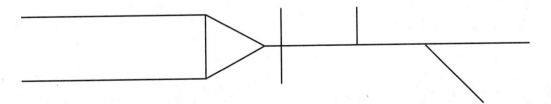

(continued)

Exercise 5 (continued) · Identify It and Diagram It

Compound Predicates

1. Sometimes, they <u>score</u> (and) <u>win</u> the game.

2. In springtime, they plow and plant crops.

3. At the airport, many planes come and go daily.

1. Sometimes, they score and win the game.

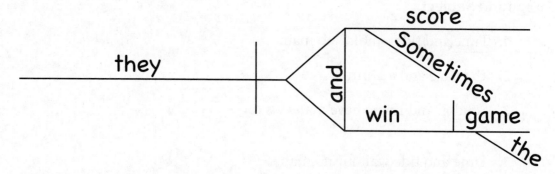

2. In springtime, they plow and plant crops.

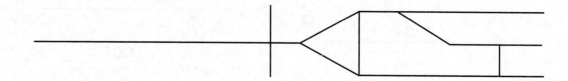

3. At the airport, many planes come and go daily.

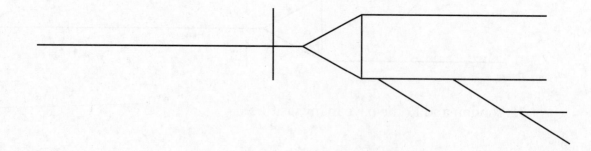

Exercise 5 (continued) · Identify It and Diagram It

Compound Direct Objects

1. They told <u>tales</u> (and) <u>jokes</u>.

2. The dome holds baseball games and football games.

3. We used red tile and white trim.

1. They told tales and jokes.

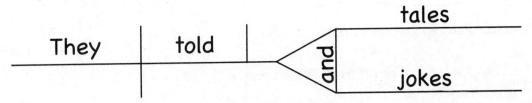

2. The dome holds baseball games and football games.

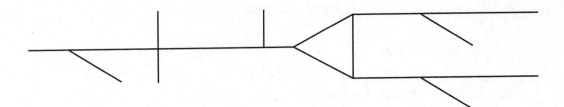

3. We used red tile and white trim.

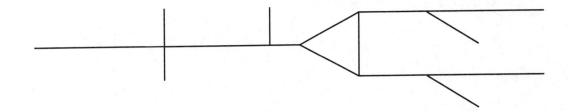

Exercise 6 · Phrase It

▸ Use the penciling strategy to "scoop" the phrases in each sentence.

▸ Read as you would speak them.

▸ The first two are done for you.

1. The globe has 24 time zones.

2. Time zone lines run from pole to pole.

3. Planes can cross many time zones.

4. A plane takes off from Wisconsin.

5. Check the time in this zone.

6. The clock inside your body is mixed up.

7. You have jet lag!

8. We have 12-hour clocks in our homes.

9. Use a 24-hour clock.

10. Can you tell time like this?

▸ Highlight or underline one-syllable words with a **final silent e**.

▸ Record five different **final silent e** words on the lines below.

Note: The word **live** does not use the long / i / sound in this selection. It is not a **final silent e** word in this context.

---

based on "It's About Time"

Where do you live? What time zone is it? The globe has 24 time zones. They are about the same size. Time zone lines run from pole to pole. The continental U.S. has four time zones. You cross from zone to zone. You must adjust the clock. Set the time up or back an hour. Take a ride. Drive west in the U.S. You drive into the next time zone. Set your clock back one hour. Drive east. You cross a time zone line as well. This time you lost an hour. Adjust your clock.

---

1. _____

2. _____

3. _____

4. _____

5. _____

Exercise 1 · Contract It

▶ Read the contractions.

▶ Draw a line to the two words that make the contraction.

1. I'll		he will
2. you'll		they will
3. she'll		we will
4. he'll		I will
5. it'll		you will
6. they'll		she will
7. we'll		it will

▶ Read each contraction.

▶ Cross out the letters that get "squeezed out" or contracted. Replace them with an apostrophe (').

▶ Rewrite each contraction.

▶ Read them again.

Read it	Cross out and replace	Rewrite it
1. I'll	I will	
2. you'll	you will	
3. she'll	she will	
4. he'll	he will	
5. it'll	it will	
6. they'll	they will	
7. we'll	we will	

Exercise 2 · Rewrite It: Present Progressive to Past

▸ Read the sentences in the first column.

▸ Change the underlined verb to past tense.

Present and Present Progressive Sentences	Past Tense Sentences
Examples:	
Lisa <u>is helping</u> him hunt for his missing math notes.	Lisa __helped__ him hunt for his missing math notes.
Nell <u>sketches</u> conch shells.	Nell __sketched__ conch shells.
The cops <u>are stopping</u> traffic to help the van with a flat.	The cops __stopped__ traffic to help the van with a flat.
1. Steve is <u>baking</u> muffins for the contest.	**1.** Steve _____ muffins for the contest.
2. He <u>likes</u> pumpkin muffins best.	**2.** He _____ pumpkin muffins best.
3. He <u>adds</u> dates and nuts to his mix.	**3.** He _____ dates and nuts to his mix.
4. The contest rules <u>state</u> no nuts.	**4.** The contest rules _____ no nuts.
5. Steve <u>whips</u> up another batch.	**5.** Steve _____ up another batch.

Unit 10 · Lesson 7

Exercise 3 · Identify It: Verb Forms

▸ Read each sentence.

▸ Underline the verb.

▸ Place an X in the column to identify the verb:

- Past tense

- Past progressive

- Present tense

- Present progressive

Sentence	Past Tense	Past Progressive	Present Tense	Present Progressive
Examples: Pete <u>stacked</u> a pile of logs.	X			
Dave and Jose are <u>chopping</u> the branches.				X
Hakim and Chad <u>pack</u> their bags for a long trip.			X	
1. This time Rosa <u>is trimming</u> the pine.				
2. The tame mules <u>give</u> rides.				
3. Han <u>passed</u> his math test.				
4. Ana <u>was shining</u> the glass globes on the lamp.				
5. Pablo <u>is tossing</u> the kite into the wind.				
6. Scott <u>is making</u> shrimp and chive dip.				
7. The sudden crash <u>stops</u> traffic.				
8. Dr. Ross <u>tests</u> the lake for toxins.				
9. People <u>were taking</u> their time to slide down the slope.				
10. Dan <u>patched</u> the tire on his bike.				

Exercise 4 · Combine It: Compound Sentences

▸ Join the pairs of base sentences below to create compound sentences using the conjunction **and**.

▸ Write the sentence on the line.

▸ The first one is done for you.

1. We hiked.
2. They ran.

We hiked and they ran.

_____

3. They made the rule.
4. We kept it.

_____

_____

5. She lives in our time zone.
6. He lives in your time zone.

_____

_____

7. They will drive to the game.
8. They will put their van in the lot.

_____

_____

9. The game will be in the dome.
10. It will be the last game.

_____

_____

(continued)

Exercise 4 (continued) · Combine It: Compound Sentences

11. The sandwiches are packed.
12. We will have them for lunch.

_____

_____

13. We will ride to the bank.
14. Mom will cash a check.

_____

_____

15. My mother asked for wind chimes.
16. I got them for her.

_____

_____

17. Maria's mom will drop me there.
18. I will help with the math contest.

_____

_____

19. He fixes clocks in his shop.
20. She helps him after school.

_____

_____

Exercise 5 · Combine It: More Compound Sentences

▸ Write each sentence on a separate strip of paper.

▸ Write the conjunction **and** on another piece of paper.

▸ Combine these sentences using the conjunction **and**.

▸ Manipulate the sentences and conjunction to make a compound sentence.

▸ Read the compound sentences to the class.

1. Take a ride.
   Drive west in the U.S.

2. Drive west in the U.S.
   Set your clock back one hour.

3. Drive east.
   You lost an hour.

4. A plane takes off from Wisconsin.
   It crosses 12 time zones.

5. The clock inside your body is mixed up.
   It takes time to adjust.

Exercise 1 · Syllable Awareness: Segmentation

▶ Listen to each word the teacher says.

▶ Count the syllables in each word. Write the number in the first column.

▶ Write the letter for each vowel sound you hear in the word.

▶ Mark each vowel with the correct diacritical mark:

- Short vowel sound with a breve (˘)

- Long vowel sound with a macron (¯)

	How many syllables do you hear?	First vowel sound	Second vowel sound
1.			
2.			
3.			
4.			
5.			
6.			
7.			
8.			
9.			
10.			

Exercise 2 · Sort It: Number of Syllables

▶ Label the columns on the **Sort It** template: **one syllable**, **two syllables**.

▶ Sort the words in the **Word Bank** by the number of syllables you hear.

▶ Write each word in the correct column.

Word Bank

baking	likes	shaped	ropes
liked	baked	liking	roping
shape	shaping	bakes	rising
timed	timing	times	ruling

One syllable	Two syllables

Unit 10 · Lesson 8

▸ Write the synonym (same or similar) for the word your teacher says.

1. law _____

2. foundation _____

3. cavity _____

4. jet _____

5. good _____

Exercise 4 · Diagram It: Compound Sentences

▸ Diagram these sentences from Lesson 7.

▸ Use the diagram to show how the simple sentences are combined into compound sentences.

▸ Use a three-section dotted line *(see below)* to join the two predicates.

▸ Write the conjunction **and** on the step of the dotted line.

▸ The first pair of sentences is diagrammed for you.

We hiked.
They ran.

1. We hiked and they ran.

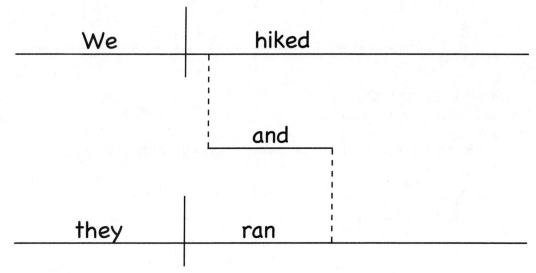

(continued)

Exercise 4 (continued) · Diagram It: Compound Sentences

They made the rule.
We kept it.

2. They made the rule **and** we kept it.

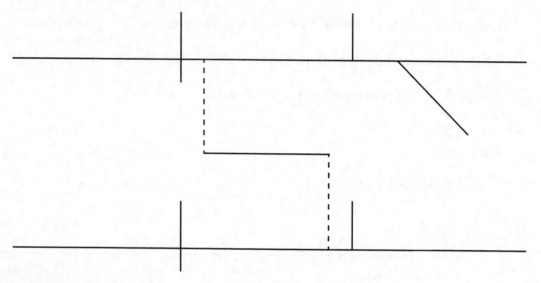

She lives in our time zone.
He lives in your time zone.

3. She lives in our time zone **and** he lives in your time zone.

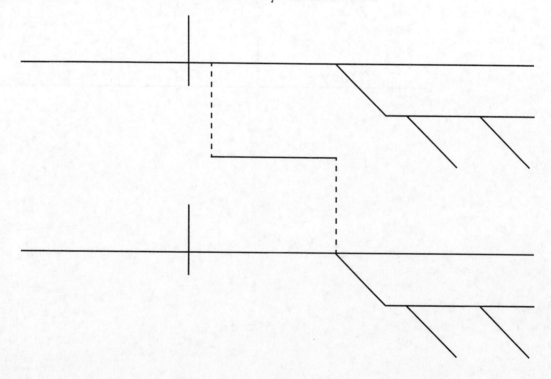

(continued)

They will drive to the game.
They will put their van in the lot.

4. They will drive to the game **and** they will put their van in the lot.

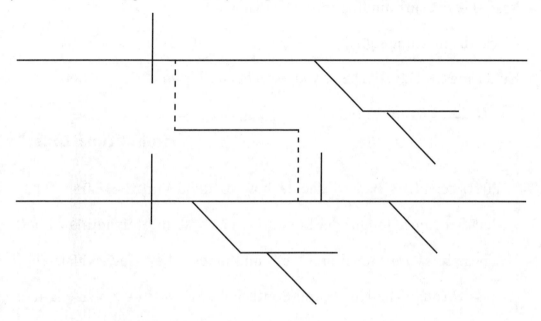

They will play the last game of the season.
They will play it in the dome.

5. They will play the last game of the season **and** they will play it in the dome.

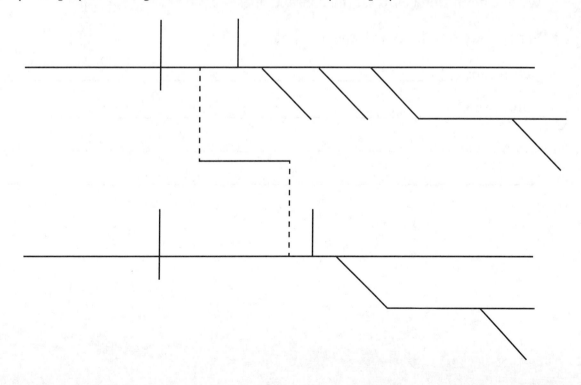

Unit 10 · Lesson 8

Exercise 5 · Use the Clues

▸ Use meaning signals and context clues to define the word **longitude**.

- Underline the vocabulary word.

- Read the text surrounding the unknown word.

- Circle the meaning signal.

- Underline the text that helps you learn about the word.

---

from "Time Zones"

First, scientists had to decide how to divide up the Earth. They decided to use longitude. Longitude is a system of imaginary lines. These lines are shown on globes and maps. They are vertical. They pass through the North and South Poles. New time zones begin at about every 15 degrees longitude.

▸ Write a definition based on the context clues.

▸ Verify your definition with the dictionary.

Definition: _____

Longitude: _____

_____

_____

Exercise 6 · Answer It

▸ Underline the signal word in each sentence.

▸ Answer each question in a complete sentence.

▸ Underline the part of the sentence that answers the question.

1. How many time zones are there?

_____

_____

2. Where in the world do time zones begin?

_____

_____

3. What is the 24-hour clock?

_____

_____

4. Identify two facts about longitude.

_____

_____

Exercise 1 · Listening for Sounds in Words

▸ Listen to each word the teacher says.

▸ Identify each vowel sound and decide if it is short or long.

▸ Mark each vowel with the correct diacritical mark.

Short = (˘)
Long = (¯)

1.	ā	e	i	o	u	oo
2.	a	ĕ	i	o	u	oo
3.	a	e	ī	o	u	oo
4.	a	e	ĭ	o	u	oo
5.	a	e	i	ō	u	oo
6.	ā	e	i	o	u	oo
7.	a	e	i	o	ŭ	oo
8.	a	e	i	o	u	o͞o
9.	a	ē	i	o	u	oo
10.	a	ĕ	i	o	u	oo

Exercise 2 · Syllable Awareness: Segmentation

▸ Listen to each word the teacher says.

▸ Count the syllables in each word. Write the number in the first column.

▸ Write the letter for each vowel sound you hear in the word.

▸ Mark the vowel with the correct diacritical mark:

- Short vowel sound with a ˘

- Long vowel sound with a ¯

	How many syllables do you hear?	First Vowel Sound	Second Vowel Sound	Third Vowel Sound
1.				
2.				
3.				
4.				
5.				
6.				
7.				
8.				
9.				
10.				

Unit 10 · Lesson 9

Exercise 3 · Sentence Dictation

▸ Listen to each sentence the teacher says.

▸ Repeat the sentence.

▸ Write it on the line.

1. _____

2. _____

3. _____

4. _____

5. _____

▸ In sentences 2, 3, and 5, find the words that have suffixes added.

▸ Write the words on the line below.

_____

▸ Rewrite sentences 1 and 4. Replace the contraction with the expanded form.

_____

_____

Exercise 4 · Find It: Verb Forms

▸ Read the verb form stated in the first column.

▸ Read the sentence in the second column.

▸ Find and underline the specified verb form in the sentence.

Find It	
Example 1: Third person singular, present tense verb	He <u>rushes</u> to get to his job on time.
Example 2: Present progressive verb	I <u>am planning</u> to run one mile every day.
	She <u>is plugging</u> her laptop into that outlet.
	They <u>are fixing</u> the pipes so we will have water.
Example 3: Past tense	People <u>depended</u> on the sun to tell time.
Example 4: Past progressive	They <u>were depending</u> on the sun to tell time.
Example 5: Future tense	He <u>will get</u> to his job on time.
1. Past tense verb	We passed through two time zones on our trip.
2. Present progressive verb	We are rushing to get back home.
3. Future tense verb	We will get to the next state in an hour.
4. Future tense verb	In that state we will pass into the next time zone.
5. Third person singular, present tense verb	The drive across time zones makes me mull over what time is.
6. Past progressive verb	In the back of the car I was thinking about time travel.
7. Future tense verb	We will have more time.
8. Future tense verb	Yet the time will change one hour on the drive east from El Paso to Dallas.
9. Present progressive verb	I am thinking that it is odd to drive across time zones.
10. Present tense verb	I get younger going west!

Unit 10 · Lesson 9

Exercise 5 · Rewrite It: Verb Forms

▶ Read the verb in the first column.

▶ Read the tense or form in the second column.

▶ Put the verb in that tense or form into the sentence.

Verb	Tense or Form	Sentence
Example 1: pass	Past	The plane just <u>passed</u> through the next time zone
Example 2: go	Past progressive	It <u>was going</u> to the next time zone.
Example 3: depend	Present	The hour <u>depends</u> on where you live.
Example 4: set	Present progressive	On the opposite side of the globe the sun <u>is setting</u>.
Example 5: rise	Future	The sun <u>will rise</u> here when it is setting there.
1. shine	future	I hope the sun _____ for the dig.
2. bring	present progressive	We _____ our lunches on the bus.
3. pack	past	I _____ a baked ham sandwich for lunch.
4. give	future	Steve _____ our class a ride to the dig site.
5. plan	present progressive	I _____ to give my lunch to Jake.
6. like	present	Jake _____ ham on a bun.
7. love	present	I _____ to eat baked ham.
8. set	future	At the dig site, we _____ up the tents.
9. camp	past progressive	Last year on the dig, we _____ out for five days.
10. want	past	All I _____ to do was to take a bath.

Exercise 6 · Draw It: Listening for Information

▸ While listening to **"Time Zones,"** sketch the three processes used to create time zones.

Using longitude to divide up the Earth | Deciding where time zones begin

Creating a 24-hour clock

Unit 10 · Lesson 9

Exercise 7 · Answer It

▸ Underline the signal word, **paraphrase**.

▸ Fill in the blanks to **paraphrase** how scientists chose longitude lines.

_____ _____ a/an _____ longitude line.

▸ Rewrite the sentence below:

_____

_____

_____

Lesson 10

Exercise 1 · Listening for Sounds in Words

▶ Listen to and repeat each pair of words the teacher says.

▶ Decide whether the vowel sound is the same or different.

▶ Mark your choice by putting an X in the correct column.

▶ If the words have the same vowel sound, write what that sound is.

	Same	Different	If they are the same, what is the vowel sound?
1.			
2.			
3.			
4.			
5.			
6.			
7.			
8.			
9.			
10.			

Check off the activities you complete with each lesson. Evaluate your accomplishments at the end of each lesson. Pay attention to teacher evaluations and comments.

Unit Objectives	Lesson 1 (Date:_____)	Lesson 2 (Date:_____)
STEP 1 — Phonemic Awareness and Phonics • Say the sounds for the consonants in these blends and clusters: l blends: bl-, cl-, fl-, gl-, pl-, sl- r blends: br-, cr-, dr-, fr-, gr-, pr-, shr-, thr-, tr- s blends: sc-, sk-, sm-, sn-, sp-, st- w blends: dw-, sw-, tw- clusters: scr-, str-, spr-, spl- • Write the letters that represent the sounds in consonant blends and clusters.	❑ Move It and Mark It ❑ Phonemic Drills ❑ See and Say ❑ Exercise 1: Say and Write ❑ Exercise 2: Listening for Sounds in Words ❑ Handwriting Practice	❑ Move It and Mark It ❑ Phonemic Drills ❑ Exercise 1: Say and Write ❑ See and Say
STEP 2 — Word Recognition and Spelling • Read and spell words with sound-spelling correspondences from this and previous units. • Read and spell the **Essential Words**: *body, each, every, know, thought, very.* • Spell words using the Drop e rule.	❑ Exercise 3: Spelling Pretest 1 ❑ Build It, Bank It ❑ Memorize It	❑ Build It, Bank It ❑ Word Fluency 1 ❑ Memorize It ❑ Handwriting Practice
STEP 3 — Vocabulary and Morphology • Define **Unit Vocabulary** words. • Identify and generate antonyms, synonyms, homophones, and attributes for **Unit Vocabulary**. • Add an apostrophe (') to plural nouns to signal plural possession.	❑ Unit Vocabulary ❑ Multiple Meaning Map (T) ❑ Expression of the Day	❑ Exercise 2: Fill In ❑ Exercise 3: Add It: Plural and Plural Possessives ❑ Exercise 4: Sort It: Singular, Plural, or Possessive Nouns ❑ Expression of the Day
STEP 4 — Grammar and Usage • Identify future progressive verb phrases. • Form compound sentences using **but**.	❑ Exercise 4: Identify It: Verbs Tell Time	❑ Exercise 5: Rewrite It: Future Progressive ❑ Exercise 6: More Rewrite It: Verb Forms
STEP 5 — Listening and Reading Comprehension • Read fluently with inflection, phrasing, and expression. • Identify time sequence organization in informational text.	❑ Exercise 5: Phrase It ❑ Decodable Text: "Facts About Kites" ❑ Exercise 6: Find It: Initial l Blends	❑ Find It: Initial l Blends ❑ Passage Fluency 1
STEP 6 — Speaking and Writing • Generate sentences that present facts. • Write a time sequence paragraph using transition words. • Answer **Understand It** questions beginning with **classify, categorize, discuss, match,** and **sort**.	❑ Masterpiece Sentences: A Six-Stage Process ❑ Sentence Types: Fact or Opinion?	❑ Exercise 7: Combine It
Self-Evaluation (5 is the highest) **Effort** = I produced my best work. **Participation** = I was actively involved in tasks. **Independence** = I worked on my own.	Effort: 1 2 3 4 5 Participation: 1 2 3 4 5 Independence: 1 2 3 4 5	Effort: 1 2 3 4 5 Participation: 1 2 3 4 5 Independence: 1 2 3 4 5
Teacher Evaluation	Effort: 1 2 3 4 5 Participation: 1 2 3 4 5 Independence: 1 2 3 4 5	Effort: 1 2 3 4 5 Participation: 1 2 3 4 5 Independence: 1 2 3 4 5

Lesson 3 (Date:_____)	Lesson 4 (Date:_____)	Lesson 5 (Date:_____)
❑ Move It and Mark It ❑ Phonemic Drills ❑ Exercise 1: Listening for Sounds in Words	❑ Move It and Mark It ❑ Phonemic Drills ❑ Exercise 1: Listening for Sounds in Words ❑ Letter-Sound Fluency	❑ Phonemic Drills ❑ Letter-Sound Fluency ❑ Exercise 1: Say and Write ❑ Content Mastery: Sound-Spelling Correspondences
❑ Build It, Bank It ❑ Drop It (T) ❑ Word Fluency 1 ❑ Exercise 2: Find It: Essential Words	❑ Build It, Bank It ❑ Word Fluency 2 ❑ Type It ❑ Handwriting Practice	❑ Content Mastery: Spelling Posttest 1 ❑ Exercise 2: Sort It: Initial Blends and Clusters
❑ Exercise 3: Word Networks: Homophones ❑ Draw It: Idioms ❑ Expression of the Day	❑ Exercise 2: Fill In ❑ Exercise 3: Add It ❑ Exercise 4: Rewrite It ❑ Expression of the Day	❑ Multiple Meaning Map (T) ❑ Expression of the Day
❑ Exercise 4: Sort It: Verb Tense	❑ Exercise 5: Tense Timeline	❑ Masterpiece Sentences: Stages 1–6 ❑ Using Masterpiece Sentences
❑ Instructional Text: "Hurricane!" ❑ Exercise 5: Use the Clues	❑ Exercise 6: Blueprint for Reading: Time Sequence Transition Words	❑ Exercise 6: Blueprint for Reading: Identifying the Details (Lesson 4)
❑ Exercise 6: Answer It	❑ Blueprint for Writing: Outline (T) ❑ Challenge Text: "The Dust Bowl"	❑ Blueprint for Writing: Adding Details to the Outline (T) ❑ Write It: Time Sequence Paragraph ❑ Challenge Text: "The Dust Bowl"
Effort: 1 2 3 4 5 Participation: 1 2 3 4 5 Independence: 1 2 3 4 5	Effort: 1 2 3 4 5 Participation: 1 2 3 4 5 Independence: 1 2 3 4 5	Effort: 1 2 3 4 5 Participation: 1 2 3 4 5 Independence: 1 2 3 4 5
Effort: 1 2 3 4 5 Participation: 1 2 3 4 5 Independence: 1 2 3 4 5	Effort: 1 2 3 4 5 Participation: 1 2 3 4 5 Independence: 1 2 3 4 5	Effort: 1 2 3 4 5 Participation: 1 2 3 4 5 Independence: 1 2 3 4 5

Check off the activities you complete with each lesson. Evaluate your accomplishments at the end of each lesson. Pay attention to teacher evaluations and comments.

Unit Objectives	Lesson 6 (Date:_____)	Lesson 7 (Date:_____)
STEP 1 **Phonemic Awareness and Phonics** • Say the sounds for the consonants in these blends and clusters: l blends: bl-, cl-, fl-, gl-, pl-, sl- r blends: br-, cr-, dr-, fr-, gr-, pr-, shr-, thr-, tr- s blends: sc-, sk-, sm-, sn-, sp-, st- w blends: dw-, sw-, tw- clusters: scr-, str-, spr-, spl- • Write the letters that represent the sounds in consonant blends and clusters.	❑ Using the Consonant and Vowel Chart ❑ Move It and Mark It ❑ Phonemic Drills ❑ See and Say ❑ Handwriting Practice ❑ Syllable Awareness: Deletion	❑ Phonemic Drills ❑ See and Name ❑ Name and Write ❑ Syllable Awareness: Segmentation
STEP 2 **Word Recognition and Spelling** • Read and spell words with sound-spelling correspondences from this and previous units. • Read and spell the **Essential Words:** *body, each, every, know, thought, very.* • Spell words using the Drop **e** rule.	❑ Exercise 1: Spelling Pretest 2 ❑ Build It, Bank It ❑ Word Fluency 3	❑ Build It, Bank It ❑ Exercise 1: Add It
STEP 3 **Vocabulary and Morphology** • Define **Unit Vocabulary** words. • Identify and generate antonyms, synonyms, homophones, and attributes for **Unit Vocabulary**. • Add an apostrophe (') to plural nouns to signal plural possession.	❑ Unit Vocabulary ❑ Exercise 2: Sort It: Semantic Categories ❑ Expression of the Day	❑ Exercise 2: Identify It: Singular or Plural Nouns or Possessives ❑ Exercise 3: Rewrite It ❑ Expression of the Day
STEP 4 **Grammar and Usage** • Identify future progressive verb phrases. • Form compound sentences using **but**.	❑ Exercise 3: Combine It	❑ Exercise 4: Expand It
STEP 5 **Listening and Reading Comprehension** • Read fluently with inflection, phrasing, and expression. • Identify time sequence organization in informational text.	❑ Exercise 4: Phrase It ❑ Decodable Text: "Kites: Shapes and Uses" ❑ Exercise 5: Find It: Final Blends	❑ Exercise 5: Find It: Final Blends (Lesson 1) ❑ Passage Fluency 2
STEP 6 **Speaking and Writing** • Generate sentences that present facts. • Write a time sequence paragraph using transition words. • Answer **Understand It** questions beginning with **classify, categorize, discuss, match,** and **sort**.	❑ Masterpiece Sentences: Compound Sentences	❑ Compound Sentences ❑ Expand It
Self-Evaluation (5 is the highest) **Effort** = I produced my best work. **Participation** = I was actively involved in tasks. **Independence** = I worked on my own.	**Effort:** 1 2 3 4 5 **Participation:** 1 2 3 4 5 **Independence:** 1 2 3 4 5	**Effort:** 1 2 3 4 5 **Participation:** 1 2 3 4 5 **Independence:** 1 2 3 4 5
Teacher Evaluation	**Effort:** 1 2 3 4 5 **Participation:** 1 2 3 4 5 **Independence:** 1 2 3 4 5	**Effort:** 1 2 3 4 5 **Participation:** 1 2 3 4 5 **Independence:** 1 2 3 4 5

Lesson 8 (Date:_____)	Lesson 9 (Date:_____)	Lesson 10 (Date:_____)
❑ Phonemic Drills ❑ Letter-Name Fluency ❑ Exercise 1: Syllable Awareness: Segmentation	❑ Phonemic Drills ❑ Exercise 1: Syllable Awareness: Segmentation ❑ Letter-Name Fluency	❑ Exercise 1: Listening for Sounds in Words
❑ Exercise 2: Listening for Word Parts ❑ Exercise 3: Build It ❑ Word Fluency 4	❑ Exercise 2: Sentence Dictation	❑ Content Mastery: Spelling Posttest 2
❑ Exercise 4: Word Networks: Antonyms, Synonyms, and Attributes ❑ Content Mastery: Word Meanings	❑ Exercise 3: Identify It: Singular, Plural, and Possessive Nouns ❑ Exercise 4: Add It ❑ Expression of the Day	❑ Exercise 2: Replace It ❑ Draw It: Idioms ❑ Expression of the Day
❑ Exercise 5: Diagram It: Compound Sentences (T)	❑ Masterpiece Sentences: Stages 1–6 ❑ Using Masterpiece Sentences: Creating Compound Sentences	❑ Content Mastery: Verb Forms/ Compound Sentences
❑ Instructional Text: "A Kite's Tale" ❑ Exercise 6: Use the Clues	❑ Exercise 5: Draw It: Listening for Information	❑ Listening for Information
❑ Exercise 7: Answer It	❑ Exercise 6: Answer It ❑ Challenge Text: "Wind Sports"	❑ Exercise 3: Blueprint for Writing: Developing Main Ideas ❑ Challenge Text: "Wind Sports"
Effort: 1 2 3 4 5 **Participation:** 1 2 3 4 5 **Independence:** 1 2 3 4 5	**Effort:** 1 2 3 4 5 **Participation:** 1 2 3 4 5 **Independence:** 1 2 3 4 5	**Effort:** 1 2 3 4 5 **Participation:** 1 2 3 4 5 **Independence:** 1 2 3 4 5
Effort: 1 2 3 4 5 **Participation:** 1 2 3 4 5 **Independence:** 1 2 3 4 5	**Effort:** 1 2 3 4 5 **Participation:** 1 2 3 4 5 **Independence:** 1 2 3 4 5	**Effort:** 1 2 3 4 5 **Participation:** 1 2 3 4 5 **Independence:** 1 2 3 4 5

Exercise 1 · Say and Write

▶ Repeat each sound your teacher says.

▶ Write the letters for the initial blend or vowel sound.

▶ Add the correct diacritical mark (breve) over the vowel letters.

1. _____ 2. _____ 3. _____ 4. _____ 5. _____

6. _____ 7. _____ 8. _____ 9. _____ 10. _____

Exercise 2 · Listening for Sounds in Words

▶ Write the letters in the box where you hear an initial **l** blend.

▶ If you hear a different blend, put an X in the first box.

1. ▯▯▯   6. ▯▯▯

2. ▯▯▯   7. ▯▯▯

3. ▯▯▯   8. ▯▯▯

4. ▯▯▯   9. ▯▯▯

5. ▯▯▯   10. ▯▯▯

Exercise 3 · Spelling Pretest 1

▶ Write each word your teacher repeats.

1. _____   6. _____   11. _____

2. _____   7. _____   12. _____

3. _____   8. _____   13. _____

4. _____   9. _____   14. _____

5. _____   10. _____   15. _____

Unit 11 · Lesson 1

Exercise 4 · Identify It: Verbs Tell Time

▶ Decide if the underlined verb or verb phrase is:

Past time

Present time

Future time

▶ Fill in the bubble to mark your answer.

▶ Do the first item with your teacher, as an example.

▶ Check and revise your answers with your teacher.

	Past	Present	Future
1. The truck <u>is blocking</u> the left lane of traffic.	◯	◯	◯
2. The store <u>will close</u> at ten.	◯	◯	◯
3. We <u>will print</u> the lists for our class sale.	◯	◯	◯
4. They <u>were skating</u> at the rink in the mall.	◯	◯	◯
5. We <u>solved</u> the problem, with his help.	◯	◯	◯
6. He <u>is acting</u> in Mr. Ming's place.	◯	◯	◯
7. She <u>will bring</u> the case to a close.	◯	◯	◯
8. The printer <u>was grabbing</u> the paper.	◯	◯	◯
9. He <u>will drive</u> tomorrow.	◯	◯	◯
10. The kite <u>is flapping</u> in the wind.	◯	◯	◯

Exercise 5 · Phrase It

▸ Use the penciling strategy to "scoop" the phrases in each sentence. Read them as you would speak them. The first two are done for you.

1. The string is tied to the kite's frame.

2. The wind lifts the kite into the air.

3. The string slips from your hand.

4. If there's wind, the kite is up.

5. The kite drifts up until it is just a speck.

6. In 200 BC, kites were not for fun.

7. Kites were used to pass thoughts.

8. In combat, kites sent coded facts.

9. The facts could help one side win.

10. Kites were used like this for a long time.

Unit 11 · Lesson 1

Exercise 6 · Find It: Initial l Blends

▸ Highlight words with **initial l blends**.

▸ Write five words with **initial l blends** on the lines below.

---

from "Facts About Kites"

In one hand is a flat stick. On the stick is lots of string. In the left hand is a block-shaped kite. The string is tied to the kite's black frame. Undo the string as you run. Let the string slide from the stick. The wind lifts the kite into the air. It glides higher and higher. The string slips from your hand. If there's wind, the kite is up. It's off! It takes skill. It takes wind. It takes luck! The kite drifts up until it is just a speck. You can get just a glimpse from the end of the string.

---

1. _____

2. _____

3. _____

4. _____

5. _____

Exercise 1 · Say and Write

▶ Repeat each sound your teacher says.

▶ Write the letters for the initial blend or vowel sound.

▶ Add the correct diacritical mark (breve) over the vowel letters.

1. _____   2. _____   3. _____   4. _____   5. _____

6. _____   7. _____   8. _____   9. _____   10. _____

Exercise 2 · Fill In

▶ Use the words in the **Answer Box** to fill in the blanks in the sentences below.

Answer Box

s'
's
suffixes
owns, has, or takes
own, have, or take

1. Both **s'** and **'s** are _____.

2. The _____ suffix is the singular possessive suffix.

3. The _____ suffix means just one person or thing

   _____.

4. The _____ suffix is the plural possessive suffix.

5. It means two or more people or things _____.

Unit 11 · Lesson 2

Exercise 3 · Add It: Plural and Plural Possessives

▸ First, make the singular noun plural by adding **s**.

▸ Next, add the apostrophe to make the plural noun into a plural possessive noun.

▸ Finally, add something that the owners might own.

Singular Noun	Plural Noun (Two or more)	Plural Possessive Noun (Two or more owners)
Examples:		
bike	bikes	bikes' tires
mom	moms	moms' dresses
1. chimp	1. chimp___	1. chimp_____
2. snake	2. snake___	2. snake_____
3. dude	3. dude___	3. dude_____
4. mule	4. mule___	4. mule_____
5. skunk	5. skunk___	5. skunk_____

Exercise 4 · Sort It: Singular, Plural, or Possessive Nouns

▶ Read the words below.

▶ Sort the examples with your teacher.

▶ Copy the words into the correct column.

▶ Say the sound as you write each letter. Say "apostrophe" when you write the apostrophe.

Examples: rabbits boss boss's scab bosses rabbit's victims' bandits'

batches	dump	scribe's
brides	mess	snake
brides'	messes	snob's
champ's	pests'	snobs
cops'	ramp	snobs'
crab's	Scott	suspects'
drugs	Scott's	

Singular Noun (Just One)	Plural Noun (Two or More)	Singular Possessive Noun (The Owner)	Plural Possessive Noun (The Owners)

Unit 11 · Lesson 2

▸ Read each verb in the first column.

▸ Rewrite the verb in the future progressive form.

Verb	Future Progressive
1. stop	
2. bring	
3. close	
4. print	
5. drive	

Exercise 6 · More Rewrite It: Verb Forms

▸ Read each sentence.

▸ Rewrite the sentence. Change the future progressive verb to the indicated verb form.

▸ Hint: progressive forms use -ing endings.

▸ Check and revise your answers with your teacher.

▸ Do the first sentence with your teacher, as an example.

CHANGE TO:

1. The bus <u>will be stopping</u> at each traffic light

past

_____

2. The store <u>will be closing</u> at ten.

present

_____

3. We <u>will be printing</u> the lists for our class sale.

past progressive

_____

4. She <u>will be bringing</u> the case to a close tomorrow.

present progressive

_____

5. He <u>will be driving</u> home tomorrow.

future

_____

Unit 11 · Lesson 2

Exercise 7 · Combine It: Compound Sentences

▸ Read the two simple sentences.

▸ Combine the two sentences using the conjunction **and**.

▸ Write the compound sentence on the line.

    1. The wind blows. The kite flies.

_____

    2. The wind lifts the kite. The kite takes off.

_____

    3. Bring the kite. Grab the string.

_____

    4. The kite's frame broke. The string got tangled.

_____

    5. Scan the sky for tree branches. Fly your kite with pride.

_____

_____

Exercise 1 · Listening for Sounds in Words

▸ Listen to each word.

▸ Write the letters for the initial blend you hear.

▸ Circle the **w** blends.

1. ☐☐☐

2. ☐☐☐

3. ☐☐☐

4. ☐☐☐

5. ☐☐☐

6. ☐☐☐

7. ☐☐☐

8. ☐☐☐

9. ☐☐☐

10. ☐☐☐

Exercise 2 · Find It: Essential Words

▸ Find the Unit 11 **Essential Words** in these sentences.

▸ Underline them. There may be more than one in a sentence.

1. Each one of you is very brave.

2. I thought you had a hot lunch.

3. Did you know my granddad?

4. Milk is the best for your body.

5. I will stop every time you ask for help.

▸ Write the **Essential Words** in the spaces.

_____   _____   _____

_____   _____   _____

Exercise 3 · Word Networks: Homophones

▶ Write the words **know** and **no** on the lines in the Venn diagram.

▶ Fill in information about both words.

▶ Identify what is the same about the two words.

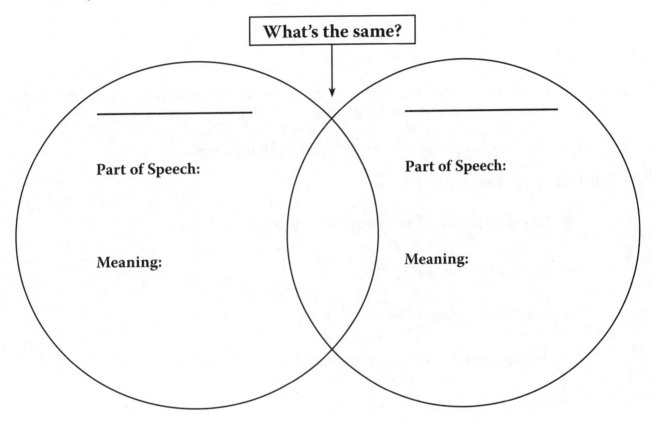

What's the same?

Part of Speech:

Meaning:

Part of Speech:

Meaning:

▶ Fill in the blanks with **know** or **no**.

1. I don't _____ your name.

2. _____ , you can't go outside.

3. I _____ how to golf.

4. _____ , I don't _____ the facts.

5. _____ parking is allowed here.

Unit 11 · Lesson 3

Exercise 4 · Sort It: Verb Tense

▸ Read the sentence and review the underlined verb or verb phrase.

▸ Decide if the underlined verbs or verb phrases are:

    Regular, past tense;

    Irregular, past tense; or

    Regular, future tense.

▸ Write the underlined verbs and verb phrases in the correct column in the chart below. **Hint:** regular past tense verbs end with -<u>ed</u>.

▸ Use your *Student Text*, page 146, for irregular verbs if needed.

▸ The first one is done as an example.

1. We <u>spent</u> the day on a trip with our classmates.

2. He <u>will adjust</u> the car's brakes.

3. Each time I <u>swung</u>, I missed the ball.

4. I <u>missed</u> the bus and had to run home.

5. Ms. Lopez <u>bent</u> the glass rod for us.

6. Congress <u>passed</u> the act in 1885.

7. Spring <u>will bring</u> sunshine and roses.

8. She <u>drank</u> a lot of milk to make her bones stronger.

9. Mom <u>brought</u> us frosted glasses of lemonade.

10. We <u>stood</u> outside, giving out prizes to the winners.

(continued)

	Regular, past tense	Irregular, past tense	Future tense
1.		spent	
2.			
3.			
4.			
5.			
6.			
7.			
8.			
9.			
10.			

Unit 11 · Lesson 3

Exercise 5 · Use the Clues

▶ Use meaning signals to define **Coriolis effect**.

▶ Underline the vocabulary word.

▶ Read the text surrounding the unknown word.

▶ Circle the meaning signal.

▶ Underline the words that help define the unknown word.

---

from "Hurricane!"

Hurricanes are not like ordinary storms. They are different. They have powerful, spinning winds. The winds rotate. They whip around the storm center. The center is the *eye* of the storm. Earth's rotation affects the direction of the spin. North of the equator, winds spin to the right. In the south, they spin to the left. This is called the *Coriolis effect*. These whirling winds are dangerous. They cause a thunderstorm to form. It will become a tropical storm. Then, it will become a hurricane.

▶ Write a definition based on the context clues.

▶ Verify your definition with the dictionary or www.yourdictionary.com.

Coriolis effect - _____

_____

_____

_____

_____

Exercise 6 · Answer It

▸ Underline the signal word in the question.

▸ Answer each question in complete sentences.

1. Categorize the kind of storm that occurs when a thunderstorm becomes an organized system.

   _____

   _____

2. Classify the kind of storm created when spinning winds top 74 mph.

   _____

   _____

3. Once a hurricane develops, describe how it finally stops.

   _____

   _____

4. Predict what kind of destruction can happen when a hurricane hits land.

   _____

   _____

   _____

5. Summarize the stages of a hurricane.
   Hint: Use your time sequence transition words to help guide your answer: **to begin, next, then, consequently, finally.**

   _____

   _____

   _____

   _____

Exercise 1 · Listening for Sounds in Words

▸ Listen to each word.

▸ Put an X to show where you hear the sound your teacher says.

1. ☐☐☐☐   6. ☐☐☐

2. ☐☐☐☐   7. ☐☐☐☐

3. ☐☐☐☐   8. ☐☐☐

4. ☐☐☐☐   9. ☐☐☐☐

5. ☐☐☐☐   10. ☐☐☐

Exercise 2 · Fill In

▸ Use the words in the **Answer Box** to fill in the blanks in the sentences below.

Answer Box

es
s' or es'
apostrophe (')
plural
s, z, x, sh, ch, or tch
own, have, or take

1. To form a plural possessive noun you first make the noun

    _____.

2. Use the plural suffix _____ for nouns that end

    _____.

3. Then you add the _____ to show possession.

4. Nouns ending in the _____ or

    _____ suffix are plural possessive nouns.

5. The plural possessive means that two or more people, animals, or things

    _____ something.

Unit 11 · Lesson 4

Exercise 3 · Add It

▸ First make the singular noun into a plural noun by adding **-es**.

▸ Then add the apostrophe (') to make the plural possessive form.

▸ Read the plural possessive phrase and complete the sentence by adding a verb phrase.

Singular Noun	Plural Noun (add the plural suffix)	Plural Possessive Noun (add the apostrophe)
boss	boss_es_	The boss_es'_ gazes _fell on Fred, who was snoring_ .
fish	fish_es_	The fish_es'_ fins _make waves_ _____ .
1. ax	1. ax___	1. The ax___ blades _____
2. class	2. class___	2. The class___ test _____
3. whiz	3. whizz___	3. The chess whizz___ games _____
4. finch	4. finch___	4. Five finch___ nests _____
5. bass	5. bass___	5. Ten bass___ fins _____

Exercise 4 · Rewrite It

▸ Underline the singular possessive word in the first sentence.

▸ Rewrite the singular possessive into a plural possessive.

▸ Read the new sentence to check your work.

Sentence with a Singular Possessive Noun	Sentence with a Plural Possessive Noun
The <u>mole's</u> hole smells damp and dank. The <u>fish's</u> fins are strong.	The ___moles'___ hole smells damp and dank. The ___fishes'___ fins are strong.
1. The storm is spinning toward the boss's cabin.	1. The storm is spinning toward the _____ cabin.
2. The wind swept sand into the camper's tent.	2. The wind swept sand into the _____ tent.
3. The finch's eggs fall from the nest.	3. The _____ eggs fall from the nest.
4. The nuthatch's nest rests in the branches.	4. The _____ nests rest in the branches.
5. The wind spun the cabin's trash all over the grass.	5. The wind spun the _____ trash all over the grass.
6. The wind makes waves on the duck's big pond.	6. The wind makes waves on the _____ big pond.
7. The ranch's fences were tossed by the wind.	7. The _____ fences were tossed by the wind.
8. Gusts of wind slash the camp's tents.	8. Gusts of wind slash the _____ tents.
9. Big drops of rain splash by the mule's pen.	9. Big drops of rain splash by the _____ pen.
10. The class's plans for the picnic came to a quick end.	10. The _____ plans for the picnic came to a quick end.

Exercise 5 · Tense Timeline

▸ Listen to each sentence that your teacher reads.

▸ Identify and write the verb or verb phrase under the correct position in each chart.

▸ Expand the verb to include five additional forms on the **Tense Timeline**. Use the model your teacher has created on the overhead transparency.

1. We **spend** a lot of time helping each other with math.

Past	Present	Future
	spend	

2. My mom **is thinking** about getting a car.

Past	Present	Future

3. They **will be standing** outside.

Past	Present	Future

4. The hurricane **hits** land.

Past	Present	Future

(continued)

Exercise 5 (continued) · **Tense Timeline**

5. The people **escaped** without harm.

Past	Present	Future

Unit 11 · Lesson 4

Exercise 6 · Blueprint for Reading: Time Sequence Transition Words

▸ Highlight the main ideas in blue.

▸ Circle the transition words: **first, next, finally**.

---

from "Hurricane!"

First, a tropical storm becomes a hurricane. Two things must be in place. They are wind strength and wind spin. First, the sustained winds must be 74 mph or higher. A sustained wind is a continuous wind. Many storms have strong wind gusts. But sustained winds are not gusting winds. They are not short winds. Second, the winds spin. They spin around the *eye*. When these two events happen, the storm has become a hurricane!

Next, the hurricane builds strength. It feeds on warm air. It feeds on moist air. It begins to move. It moves between 10 and 50 miles per hour. The towering clouds form a wind wall. This wall holds the strongest winds. It holds the heaviest rains. The wall surrounds the eye. The strong winds spin wildly. They whirl around the *eye*. Their speeds are intense! They sometimes get up to 200 miles an hour. If the hurricane hits land, flooding and destruction follow.

Finally, the hurricane ends. The hurricane hits an area of cool land or water. It enters a cold, unfriendly surrounding. It loses its supply of hot, moist air. There is nothing to feed it. The *eye* disappears. The storm is dead.

Exercise 7 · Blueprint for Writing: Outline

_____

Main Idea

I. _____

    A. _____

    B. _____

    C. _____

    D. _____

Main Idea

II. _____

    A. _____

    B. _____

    C. _____

    D. _____

Main Idea

III. _____

    A. _____

    B. _____

    C. _____

    D. _____

Conclusion _____

Exercise 1 · Say and Write

▸ Repeat the sounds your teacher says.

▸ Write the letters for the sounds.

1. _____   2. _____   3. _____   4. _____   5. _____

6. _____   7. _____   8. _____   9. _____   10. _____

Exercise 2 · Sort It: Initial Blends and Clusters

▸ Sort the words according to their initial blend or cluster.

▸ Write the words in columns according to the sort.

black	brake	smoke	twin
dwell	scrap	stick	stroke
thrill	bring	spring	flame

l-blends	**r**-blends	**s**-blends	**w**-blends	clusters

1. Which word has a digraph?

_____

2. What is the difference between a digraph and a blend?

_____

_____

Exercise 1 · Spelling Pretest 2

▸ Write the words your teacher says.

1. _____   6. _____   11. _____

2. _____   7. _____   12. _____

3. _____   8. _____   13. _____

4. _____   9. _____   14. _____

5. _____   10. _____   15. _____

Exercise 2 · Sort It: Semantic Categories

▸ Read the words in the **Word Bank**.

▸ Sort the words into categories.

▸ Some words may be used twice.

Word Bank

crash	swing	cast
champ	skate	broke
cast	bride	block
dent	class	witch
swim	crutch	punt

People	Sport Actions	Accident

Exercise 3 · Combine It

▸ Read each sentence pair.

▸ Decide whether to use the conjunction *and* or *but* to create a compound sentence.

▸ Write the new sentence on the line.

▸ Circle the conjunction, *and* or *but*, that you use to join your compound sentence.

▸ Use a comma before the conjunction.

▸ Review sentences with your teacher, and make necessary corrections.

1. They suggested evacuation before the storm. Many did not leave.

_____

_____

2. The eye is the center of the hurricane. The winds spin around the eye.

_____

_____

3. Everything is still in the eye. Strong winds come back after that.

_____

_____

4. Hurricanes are predicted days ahead of time. Some people do not prepare.

_____

_____

5. Hurricanes cause much damage. People need to find a safe place.

_____

_____

(continued)

6. Long ago there were no meteorologists. Hurricanes surprised people.

_____

_____

7. Some people have no defense in the storm. They can go to shelters.

_____

_____

8. Much work is needed after a hurricane. Some people will not help.

_____

_____

9. After a hurricane, some will give up hope. Some stay strong.

_____

_____

10. We will do our planning before the storm. We may still have damage.

_____

_____

Exercise 4 · Phrase It

▸ Using the penciling strategy, "scoop" the phrases in each sentence. Read them as you would speak them. The first two are done for you.

1. Kites have many shapes and uses.

2. The frame is shaped like a cross.

3. Cloth or plastic is put on the frame.

4. Kites can have long tails.

5. Without a tail, the diamond kite spins.

6. Its shape lets it fly and not spin.

7. The shape of a kite and its use are linked.

8. Kites have been used in combat.

9. We know they sent coded facts.

10. In fact, kites have had many uses.

Exercise 5 · Find It: Final Blends

▶ Highlight or underline words with **final blends**.

▶ Record five words with **final blends** on the lines below.

> **from "Kites: Shapes and Uses"**
>
> Kites have been used in combat. We know they sent coded facts. In fact, kites have had many uses. They have helped us grasp things about our planet. How hot is it up in the sky? In the past, kites have helped us know about the sky. One string held many kites. A strong wind lifted them up. When all the kites landed, they had the facts.

1. _____

2. _____

3. _____

4. _____

5. _____

Exercise 1 · Add It

▸ Read the word.

▸ Read the suffix.

▸ Mark an X in the column of the spelling rule you need to use.

▸ Apply the spelling rule and write the new word.

	Base verb	Suffix	Double It	Drop It	No rule	Base verb + Suffix
1.	spin	ing				
2.	ask	ed				
3.	trap	ing				
4.	gripe	ing				
5.	brake	ing				
6.	pump	ed				
7.	skate	ed				
8.	grip	ing				
9.	sand	ing				
10.	state	ed				

When do we use **Double It** ?

_____

_____

When do we use **Drop It** ?

_____

_____

Exercise 2 · Identify It: Singular or Plural Nouns

▸ Read each sentence.

▸ Then place an X in the column that describes whether the underlined word is:

- A singular noun: no suffix

- A plural noun using **-s** or **-es** as a suffix

- A singular possessive noun using **'s** as a suffix

- A plural possessive noun using **s'** or **es'** as a suffix

Sentence	Singular Noun	Plural Noun	Singular Possessive Noun	Plural Possessive Noun
The <u>fan</u> broke.	X			
The <u>fans</u> broke.		X		
The <u>fan's</u> blade broke.			X	
The <u>fans'</u> blades broke.				X
1. The <u>wind's</u> gusts bent the branches.				
2. The <u>tribes'</u> lands are vast.				
3. Scott picked up the <u>finches'</u> nest.				
4. The hurricane's <u>strength</u> was not predicted.				
5. The car's <u>brakes</u> did not pass the test.				
6. <u>Kites'</u> shapes and sizes can change.				
7. The <u>wind</u> helps kites lift up into the sky.				
8. The <u>plane's</u> wings shone in the sun.				
9. The picnic was held on the <u>pond's</u> banks.				

(continued)

Exercise 2 (continued) · **Identify It: Singular or Plural Nouns**

Sentence	Singular Noun	Plural Noun	Singular Possessive Noun	Plural Possessive Noun
10. We thought Juan's <u>tricks</u> were the best.				

Exercise 3 · Rewrite It

▸ Read each sentence in the first column below.

▸ Change the underlined word to the new form listed in the middle column.

▸ Write the word in the blank.

▸ Read the new sentence.

▸ Remember, when forming the plural possessive (more than one owner):
First make the singular noun into a plural noun by adding **-s** or **-es**.
Then add the ' to make the plural possessive.

First Sentence	New Form	New Sentence
Example: The <u>crabs'</u> legs are tapping and clacking on the rocks.	Singular Possessive	The ____crab's____ legs are tapping and clacking on the rocks.
Example: The <u>foxes'</u> fur is soft and red.	Singular Possessive	The ____fox's____ fur is soft and red.
Example: The <u>fish's</u> fins are pink and black.	Plural Possessive	The ____fishes'____ fins are pink and black.
Example: The <u>plant's</u> branches are thick and strong.	Plural Possessive	The ____plants'____ branches are thick and strong.
1. The <u>brushes'</u> shafts are made of plastic.	Singular Possessive	The _____ shafts are made of plastic.
2. The <u>kite's</u> shape helps it fly.	Plural Possessive	The _____ shapes help them fly.
3. The <u>match's</u> flame lit up the tent.	Plural Possessive	The _____ flames lit up the tent.
4. The <u>storms'</u> winds can smash glass.	Singular Possessive	The _____ winds can smash glass.
5. The <u>elms'</u> branches gave us shade.	Singular Possessive	The _____ branches gave us shade.

(continued)

First Sentence	New Form	New Sentence
6. The tent's strength was tested by the wind.	Plural Possessive	The _____ strength was tested by the wind.
7. The <u>plant's</u> stems snapped in the wind gusts.	Plural Possessive	The _____ stems snapped in the wind gusts.
8. Han picked up the pop for the <u>classes'</u> picnic.	Singular Possessive	Han picked up the pop for the _____ picnic.
9. The <u>lamp's</u> glass was smashed and the poles were bent.	Plural Possessive	The _____ glass was smashed and the poles were bent.
10. It is a disaster when the <u>storms'</u> winds get up to 100 miles per hour.	Singular Possessive	It is a disaster when the _____ winds get up to 100 miles per hour.

Exercise 4 · Expand It

▶ Read each sentence.

▶ On the first line, write another sentence to expand the idea of the first sentence.

▶ Combine the two sentences into a compound sentence using **and** or **but**.

▶ Write the new compound sentence on the line.

▶ Review your compound sentences with your teacher.

1. Everybody loves kites.

_____

_____

2. The first kite was invented in China.

_____

_____

3. People use kites for experiments.

_____

_____

4. Benjamin Franklin flew a kite.

_____

_____

5. Australian Lawrence Hargrave invented the box kite.

_____

_____

Exercise 1 • Syllable Awareness: Segmentation

▸ Listen to the word the teacher says.

▸ Repeat the word and count the syllables.

▸ Write the number of syllables and the letter for each vowel sound you hear.

▸ Remember to use the proper diacritical mark.

	How many syllables do you hear?	First Vowel Sound	Second Vowel Sound	Third Vowel Sound
1.				
2.				
3.				
4.				
5.				
6.				
7.				
8.				
9.				
10.				

Exercise 2 · Listening for Word Parts

▶ Listen to each word the teacher says.

▶ Write the word part that the teacher repeats.

1. _____   2. _____   3. _____   4. _____   5. _____

6. _____   7. _____   8. _____   9. _____   10. _____

Exercise 3 · Build It

▶ Use the word parts from Exercise 2, **Listening to Word Parts**, to build as many new words as possible.

_____   _____

_____   _____

_____   _____

_____   _____

Unit 11 · Lesson 8

Exercise 4 · Word Networks: Antonyms, Synonyms, and Attributes

▸ Listen to each pair of words.

▸ Think: How are these words related?

- Opposite meanings are antonyms.

- The same or similar meanings are synonyms.

- Features, such as size, shape, or action, are attributes.

▸ Put an X in the column to show the relationship.

Word pair	Antonym	Synonym	Attribute
1. ask: tell			
2. grasp: grab			
3. skunk: stripe			
4. fresh: rotten			
5. plate: glass			
6. plate: dish			
7. send: receive			
8. wig: blond			
9. close: shut			
10. fast: quick			

Exercise 5 · Diagram It

▸ Underline the two sentences; circle the conjunction.

▸ Diagram the first sentence with your teacher.

▸ Diagram the remaining compound sentences.

▸ Review your diagrams with your teacher, and make adjustments.

1. Everybody loves kites, but some people have never flown a kite.

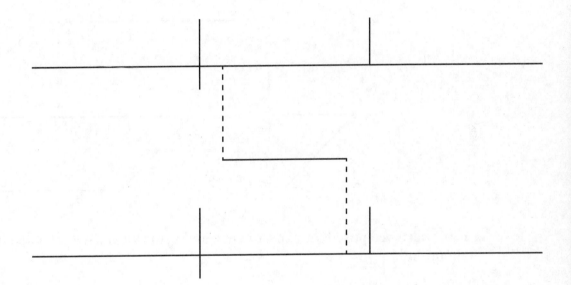

(continued)

Exercise 5 (continued) · Diagram It

2. The first kite was invented in China, but many changes have been made since then.

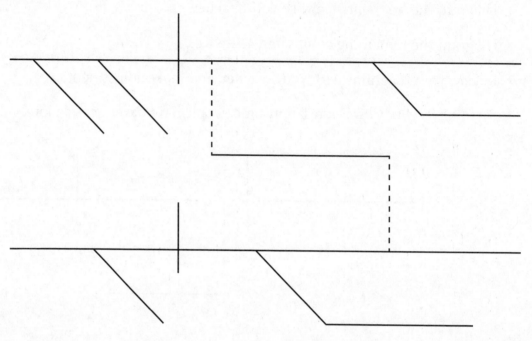

3. Kites have been used for experiments, and some kites have provided information about flight.

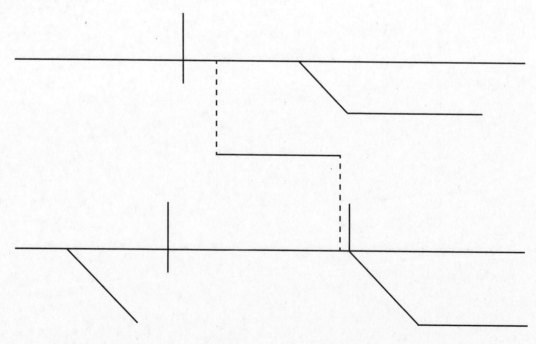

(continued)

Exercise 5 (continued) · **Diagram It**

4. Benjamin Franklin flew a kite, but the people did not understand his experiment.

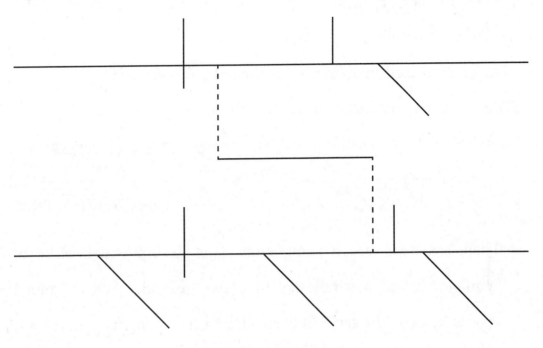

5. Lawrence Hargrave invented the box kite, and the box structure had more stability.

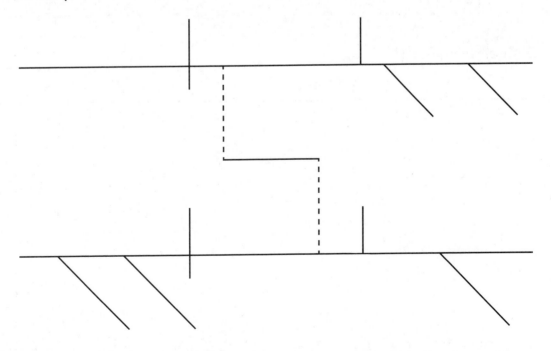

Unit 11 · Lesson 8

Exercise 6 · Use the Clues

▸ Use context clues to define the word **thermometer**.

- Circle the vocabulary word.

- Read text surrounding the unknown word.

- Underline the words that help define the unknown word.

- Write a definition based on the context clues.

- Verify your definition with the dictionary or www.yourdictionary.com.

---

from "A Kite's Tale"

Then, scientists began using kites. One example took place in Scotland. It was a windy day in 1749. Alexander Wilson joined several kites on the same line. He lifted a thermometer into the air. He measured the air temperature. He did this again, at different altitudes.

Define: thermometer - _____

_____

Exercise 7 · Answer It

▶ Underline the signal word.

▶ Answer in complete sentences.

1. Discuss the Chinese general's plan to use a kite for military use. Do you think his plan worked? How do you know from reading this article?

_____

_____

_____

_____

_____

2. List different ways kites have been used. Add your own ideas to those from the article.

1. _____   6. _____   11. _____

2. _____   7. _____   12. _____

3. _____   8. _____   13. _____

4. _____   9. _____   14. _____

5. _____   10. _____   15. _____

3. Sort the list from question 2 into categories according to how they are used.

Military Use	Scientific Use	To Study Flight	For Fun

Exercise 1 · Syllable Awareness: Segmentation

▶ Listen to each word the teacher says.

▶ Repeat the word and count the syllables.

▶ Write the number of syllables and the letter for each vowel sound you hear.

▶ Remember to use the proper diacritical mark.

	How many syllables do you hear?	First Vowel Sound	Second Vowel Sound	Third Vowel Sound
1.				
2.				
3.				
4.				
5.				
6.				
7.				
8.				
9.				
10.				

Exercise 2 · Sentence Dictation

▸ Listen to each sentence the teacher says.

▸ Repeat the sentence.

▸ Write it on the line.

1. _____

2. _____

3. _____

4. _____

5. _____

▸ Reread sentences 1–5.

▸ Find words that follow the **Doubling** rule.

▸ Write them on the line.

_____

▸ Find words that follow the **Drop e** rule.

▸ Write them on the top lines.

▸ Go back to the base for each word. Write the base words on the line below.

_____   _____   _____

_____   _____   _____

Unit 11 · Lesson 9

Exercise 3 · Identify It: Singular, Plural, and Possessive Nouns

▸ Read each sentence.

▸ Then place an X in the column that tells whether the underlined word is:

A singular noun
A plural noun
A singular possessive noun
A plural possessive noun

Sentence	Singular Noun	Plural Noun	Singular Possessive Noun	Plural Possessive Noun
The <u>fan</u> broke.	X			
The <u>fans</u> broke.		X		
The <u>fish's</u> tank is small.			X	
The <u>fishes'</u> tank is small.				X
1. Many <u>storms</u> gather strength over hot land.				
2. The <u>bosses'</u> comments will make you smile.				
3. There were two <u>skunks</u> sitting on the path.				
4. We were shocked by the cost of Al's <u>van</u>.				
5. Lisa fixed the gaskets on the <u>cops'</u> trucks.				
6. The men ate <u>Hakim's</u> muffins for lunch.				
7. Fred's backpack is still full of <u>papers</u> from his last class.				
8. The <u>mustang's</u> strength astonished us all.				
9. The skate's <u>blade</u> cut the strap.				
10. The <u>plank's</u> span stretched across the path.				

Exercise 4 · Add It

▸ Add -**s** or -**es** to singular nouns to make plural nouns.

▸ Next add the ' (apostrophe) to make the plural possessive form.

▸ Read the plural possessive phrase.

▸ With your teacher, complete the sentence by adding a verb phrase orally.

Singular Noun	Plural Noun (Add the plural suffix)	Plural Possessive Noun (Add the apostrophe)
Examples: match	match**es**	The match**es'** flames ... lit up the tent.
plane	plane**s**	The plane**s'** wings ... dipped.
1. box	box___	The box___ strength
2. disk	disk___	The disk___ black backs
3. chimp	chimp___	The chimp___ legs
4. dish	dish___	The dish___ sizes
5. bride	brid___	The bride___ dresses
6. class	class___	The class___ students
7. quiz	quizz___	The quizz___ contents
8. flag	flag___	The flag___ stripes
9. frog	frog___	The frog___ legs
10. camp	camp___	The camp___ rules

Unit 11 · Lesson 9

Exercise 5 · Draw It: Listening for Information

▸ While listening to **"A Kite's Tale,"** quickly sketch the different ways that kites have been used throughout history.

(continued)

Exercise 5 (continued) · Draw It: Listening for Information

▸ Match the sequence of events in the second column below to the time sequence transition words in the first column.

_____At first	a.	scientists began using kites
_____Later	b.	kites were used to drop information fliers
_____Then	c.	kites are used for fun
_____A little later	d.	kites were used for military use
_____Today	e.	kites were used to study flight

Exercise 6 · Answer It: Comprehension

▸ Write an answer for the question: Paraphrase how kites are used today.

▸ Use replacement words listed with your teacher.

▸ Fill in the blanks to paraphrase how kites are used today.

_____, kites are _____ for _____.

_____, kites are _____ for _____.

▸ Rewrite the sentence below:

_____

_____

Exercise 1 · Listening for Sounds in Words

▸ Write the letters for the sounds you hear in each word. Write the letter for one sound per box.

▸ Put a diacritical mark over the vowels.

▸ Circle the words with **initial** blends.

▸ Put a box around the words with **final** blends.

1.

2.

3.

4.

5.

6.

7.

8.

9.

10.

Exercise 2 · Replace It

▶ Listen to your teacher reread part of **"A Kite's Tale."**

▶ Replace the underlined words with a synonym or a word that means almost the same.

▶ Write the synonyms on the lines below.

▶ Reread the text with the synonyms.

---

from "A Kite's Tale"

Everybody <u>loves</u> kites. For more than 2,000 years, people have flown
₁

kites on <u>windy</u> days. One <u>tale</u> says that the *first* kite was <u>invented</u> in
₂   ₃   ₄

China. A wind gust <u>blew</u> off a farmer's hat.
₅

---

1. _____

2. _____

3. _____

4. _____

5. _____

Unit 11 · Lesson 10

Exercise 3 · Blueprint for Writing: Developing Main Ideas

Topic _____

I. _____

Main
Idea
    A. _____

    B. _____

    C. _____

    D. _____

II. _____

Main
Idea
    A. _____

    B. _____

III. _____

Main
Idea
    A. _____

    B. _____

    C. _____

Check off the activities you complete with each lesson. Evaluate your accomplishments at the end of each lesson. Pay attention to teacher evaluations and comments.

Unit Objectives	Lesson 1 (Date:_____)	Lesson 2 (Date:_____)
STEP 1 **Phonemic Awareness and Phonics** • Say the sounds for the consonants and consonant combinations including digraphs, trigraphs, blends, and clusters. • Write the letters for the sounds in consonant digraphs, trigraphs, blends, and clusters. • Say the short and long vowel sounds. • Write the letters for short and long vowels.	❑ Move It and Mark It ❑ Phonemic Drills ❑ See and Say ❑ Exercise 1: Say and Write ❑ Exercise 2: Listening for Sounds in Words ❑ Handwriting Practice	❑ Phonemic Drills ❑ Exercise 1: Say and Write ❑ See and Say ❑ Exercise 2: Listening for Sounds in Words ❑ Exercise 3: Count It
STEP 2 **Word Recognition and Spelling** • Read and spell words with sound-spelling correspondences from this and previous units. • Read and spell contractions: not, will, would. • Read and spell the **Essential Words**: Dr., Mr., Mrs., Ms., find, only. • Spell words with **Doubling** and **Drop e Rules**.	❑ Exercise 3: Spelling Pretest 1 ❑ Build It, Bank It ❑ Memorize It	❑ Build It, Bank It ❑ Word Fluency 1 ❑ Introduction: Abbreviations ❑ Memorize It ❑ Handwriting Practice
STEP 3 **Vocabulary and Morphology** • Define **Unit Vocabulary** words. • Generate synonyms, antonyms, attributes, and homophones for **Unit Vocabulary**. • Use suffixes to form noun plurals, possessives, and verb tenses.	❑ Unit Vocabulary ❑ Multiple Meaning Map (T) ❑ Expression of the Day	❑ Exercise 4: Fill In: Suffixes and Tenses ❑ Exercise 5: Rewrite It: Verb Tenses ❑ Expression of the Day
STEP 4 **Grammar and Usage** • Identify nouns as subjects, direct objects, and objects of a preposition in sentences. • Identify verb tenses: past, present, and future. • Identify compound subjects, predicates, direct objects, and sentences.	❑ Exercise 4: Find It: Nouns ❑ Exercise 5: Sort It: Noun Categories	❑ Exercise 6: Identify It: Noun Functions
STEP 5 **Listening and Reading Comprehension** • Identify time sequence organization in informational text. • Select context clues from informational text.	❑ Exercise 6: Phrase It ❑ Decodable Text: "What's for Lunch?" ❑ Exercise 7: Find It: Short Vowels	❑ Exercise 7: Find It: Short Vowels (Lesson 1) ❑ Passage Fluency 1
STEP 6 **Speaking and Writing** • Generate sentences that present facts. • Write a time sequence paragraph using transition words. • Answer **Understand It** questions.	❑ Exercise 8: Masterpiece Sentences	❑ Masterpiece Sentences: Stages 1 and 2
Self-Evaluation (5 is the highest) **Effort** = I produced my best work. **Participation** = I was actively involved in tasks. **Independence** = I worked on my own.	Effort: 1 2 3 4 5 Participation: 1 2 3 4 5 Independence: 1 2 3 4 5	Effort: 1 2 3 4 5 Participation: 1 2 3 4 5 Independence: 1 2 3 4 5
Teacher Evaluation	Effort: 1 2 3 4 5 Participation: 1 2 3 4 5 Independence: 1 2 3 4 5	Effort: 1 2 3 4 5 Participation: 1 2 3 4 5 Independence: 1 2 3 4 5

Lesson 3 (Date:_____)	Lesson 4 (Date:_____)	Lesson 5 (Date:_____)
❑ Move It and Mark It ❑ Phonemic Drills ❑ Exercise 1: Listening for Sounds in Words	❑ Move It and Mark It ❑ Phonemic Drills ❑ Exercise 1: Listening for Sounds in Words ❑ Letter-Sound Fluency	❑ Phonemic Drills ❑ Letter-Sound Fluency ❑ Exercise 1: Say and Write
❑ Exercise 2: Listening for Word Parts ❑ Double It (T) ❑ Word Fluency 1 ❑ Exercise 3: Find It: Essential Words	❑ Chain It (T) ❑ Word Fluency 2 ❑ Type It: Essential Words ❑ Handwriting Practice	❑ Content Mastery: Spelling Posttest 1 ❑ Exercise 2: Consonant Review ❑ Exercise 3: Sort It: Consonant Combinations
❑ Exercise 4: Word Networks: Homophones ❑ Draw It: Idioms ❑ Expression of the Day	❑ Exercise 2: Fill In: Noun Suffixes ❑ Exercise 3: Rewrite It: Noun Suffixes ❑ Exercise 4: More Rewrite It: Noun Suffixes ❑ Expression of the Day	❑ Multiple Meaning Map (T) ❑ Expression of the Day
❑ Exercise 5: Verb Tense Review ❑ Exercise 6: Identify It: Irregular Past Tense Verbs	❑ Exercise 5: Tense Timeline	❑ Masterpiece Sentences: Noun and Pronoun Functions
❑ Instructional Text: "Making Hero Sandwiches" ❑ Exercise 7: Use the Clues	❑ Exercise 6: Blueprint for Reading: Time Sequence Transition Words	❑ Blueprint for Reading: Identifying the Details
❑ Exercise 8: Answer It	❑ Exercise 7: Blueprint for Writing: Outline (T) ❑ Challenge Text: "Sandwiches + Hero = Success"	❑ Blueprint for Writing: Adding Details to the Outline (T) ❑ Write It: Answering Questions Using the Outline ❑ Challenge Text: "Sandwiches + Hero = Success"
Effort: 1 2 3 4 5 **Participation:** 1 2 3 4 5 **Independence:** 1 2 3 4 5	**Effort:** 1 2 3 4 5 **Participation:** 1 2 3 4 5 **Independence:** 1 2 3 4 5	**Effort:** 1 2 3 4 5 **Participation:** 1 2 3 4 5 **Independence:** 1 2 3 4 5
Effort: 1 2 3 4 5 **Participation:** 1 2 3 4 5 **Independence:** 1 2 3 4 5	**Effort:** 1 2 3 4 5 **Participation:** 1 2 3 4 5 **Independence:** 1 2 3 4 5	**Effort:** 1 2 3 4 5 **Participation:** 1 2 3 4 5 **Independence:** 1 2 3 4 5

Check off the activities you complete with each lesson. Evaluate your accomplishments at the end of each lesson. Pay attention to teacher evaluations and comments.

Unit Objectives	Lesson 6 (Date:_____)	Lesson 7 (Date:_____)
STEP 1 **Phonemic Awareness and Phonics** • Say the sounds for the consonants and consonant combinations including digraphs, trigraphs, blends, and clusters. • Write the letters for the sounds in consonant digraphs, trigraphs, blends, and clusters. • Say the short and long vowel sounds. • Write the letters for short and long vowels.	❑ Using the Vowel Chart (T) ❑ Move It and Mark It ❑ Phonemic Drills ❑ Listening for Sounds in Words ❑ See and Say ❑ Exercise 1: Say and Write ❑ Handwriting Practice	❑ Phonemic Drills ❑ Exercise 1: Listening for Sounds in Words
STEP 2 **Word Recognition and Spelling** • Read and spell words with sound-spelling correspondences from this and previous units. • Read and spell contractions: not, will, would. • Read and spell the **Essential Words**: *Dr., Mr., Mrs., Ms., find, only.* • Spell words with **Doubling** and **Drop e Rules**.	❑ Exercise 2: Spelling Pretest 2 ❑ Build It, Bank It ❑ Word Fluency 3	❑ Build It, Bank It ❑ Drop It: Drop <u>e</u> (T)
STEP 3 **Vocabulary and Morphology** • Define **Unit Vocabulary** words. • Generate synonyms, antonyms, attributes, and homophones for **Unit Vocabulary**. • Use suffixes to form noun plurals, possessives, and verb tenses.	❑ Unit Vocabulary ❑ Exercise 3: Sort It: Meaning Categories ❑ Expression of the Day	❑ Exercise 2: Rewrite It: Verbs ❑ Exercise 3: Find It: Verb Forms ❑ Exercise 4: Find It: Noun Suffixes ❑ Expression of the Day
STEP 4 **Grammar and Usage** • Identify nouns as subjects, direct objects, and objects of a preposition in sentences. • Identify verb tenses: past, present, and future. • Identify compound subjects, predicates, direct objects, and sentences.	❑ Exercise 4: Expand It: Compound Parts	❑ Exercise 5: Combine It: Compound Sentence Parts
STEP 5 **Listening and Reading Comprehension** • Identify time sequence organization in informational text. • Select context clues from informational text.	❑ Instructional Text: "Eponymous Sandwiches" ❑ Exercise 5: Use the Clues	❑ Exercise 6: Draw It: Listening for Information
STEP 6 **Speaking and Writing** • Generate sentences that present facts. • Write a time sequence paragraph using transition words. • Answer **Understand It** questions.	❑ Exercise 6: Answer It	❑ Exercise 7: Answer It ❑ Challenge Text: "A World of Sandwiches"
Self-Evaluation (5 is the highest) **Effort** = I produced my best work. **Participation** = I was actively involved in tasks. **Independence** = I worked on my own.	**Effort:** 1 2 3 4 5 **Participation:** 1 2 3 4 5 **Independence:** 1 2 3 4 5	**Effort:** 1 2 3 4 5 **Participation:** 1 2 3 4 5 **Independence:** 1 2 3 4 5
Teacher Evaluation	**Effort:** 1 2 3 4 5 **Participation:** 1 2 3 4 5 **Independence:** 1 2 3 4 5	**Effort:** 1 2 3 4 5 **Participation:** 1 2 3 4 5 **Independence:** 1 2 3 4 5

Lesson 8 (Date:_____)	Lesson 9 (Date:_____)	Lesson 10 (Date:_____)
❏ Phonemic Drills ❏ Letter-Name Fluency ❏ Exercise 1: Syllable Awareness: Segmentation	❏ Phonemic Drills ❏ Exercise 1: Syllable Awareness: Segmentation ❏ Letter-Name Fluency ❏ Handwriting Practice	❏ Summative Test: Phonemic Awareness and Phonics
❏ Exercise 2: Contract It ❏ Word Fluency 4 ❏ Progress Indicators: Test of Silent Word Reading Fluency (TOSWRF)	❏ Progress Indicators: Spelling Inventory	❏ Content Mastery: Spelling Posttest 2
❏ Exercise 3: Classify It	(Spelling Inventory Test, continued)	❏ Summative Test: Vocabulary and Morphology
❏ Exercise 4: Diagram It: Compound Parts (T)	❏ Masterpiece Sentences: Stages 1–6 ❏ Using Masterpiece Sentences: Creating Sentences With Compound Parts ❏ Exercise 2: Find It: Nouns	❏ Summative Test: Grammar and Usage
❏ Listening for Information: Instructional Text: "Eponymous Sandwiches"	(Summative Test: Composition)	❏ Progress Indicators: Degrees of Reading Power (DRP)
❏ Exercise 5: Blueprint for Writing: Developing Main Ideas ❏ Challenge Text: "A World of Sandwiches"	❏ Summative Test: Composition	(Degrees of Reading Power Test, continued)
Effort: 1 2 3 4 5 **Participation:** 1 2 3 4 5 **Independence:** 1 2 3 4 5	**Effort:** 1 2 3 4 5 **Participation:** 1 2 3 4 5 **Independence:** 1 2 3 4 5	**Effort:** 1 2 3 4 5 **Participation:** 1 2 3 4 5 **Independence:** 1 2 3 4 5
Effort: 1 2 3 4 5 **Participation:** 1 2 3 4 5 **Independence:** 1 2 3 4 5	**Effort:** 1 2 3 4 5 **Participation:** 1 2 3 4 5 **Independence:** 1 2 3 4 5	**Effort:** 1 2 3 4 5 **Participation:** 1 2 3 4 5 **Independence:** 1 2 3 4 5

Exercise 1 · Say and Write

▸ Write the letter or letters for each sound your teacher says.

▸ Say the sounds as you write the letters.

▸ Add the correct diacritical mark (breve) over the vowel letter to signal the short vowel sound.

1. _____ 2. _____ 3. _____ 4. _____ 5. _____

6. _____ 7. _____ 8. _____ 9. _____ 10. _____

Exercise 2 · Listening for Sounds in Words

▸ Write the letters that represent the digraph you hear in each word.

1. _____ 2. _____ 3. _____ 4. _____ 5. _____

6. _____ 7. _____ 8. _____ 9. _____ 10. _____

Exercise 3 · Spelling Pretest 1

▸ Write the words your teacher says.

1. _____   6. _____   11. _____
2. _____   7. _____   12. _____
3. _____   8. _____   13. _____
4. _____   9. _____   14. _____
5. _____   10. _____   15. _____

Exercise 4 · Find It: Nouns

▸ Go to the **Unit Vocabulary** list in your *Student Text*, page 178.

▸ Find 20 words that can be used as nouns.

▸ List them here.

1. _____   6. _____   11. _____   16. _____
2. _____   7. _____   12. _____   17. _____
3. _____   8. _____   13. _____   18. _____
4. _____   9. _____   14. _____   19. _____
5. _____   10. _____   15. _____   20. _____

Unit 12 · Lesson 1

Exercise 5 · Sort It: Noun Categories

▸ Review your noun lists from Exercise 4, **Find It: Nouns**.

▸ Preview the four categories in the chart below (*people, places, things,* and *ideas*).

- Write each of your 20 nouns in the appropriate column.

- If you find a word that does not fit in any column, cross it off your list and find a replacement word from the **Unit Vocabulary**.

- Make sure you list 20 nouns in the chart below.

- Use a dictionary if needed.

▸ Review your nouns with your teacher to ensure that they are in the right columns.

People	Places	Things	Ideas

(continued)

Exercise 5 (continued) · Sort It: Noun Categories

People	Places	Things		Ideas

Exercise 6 · Phrase It

▸ Use the penciling strategy to "scoop" the phrases in each sentence.

▸ Read as you would speak them.

▸ The first two are done for you.

1. Most of us take time for lunch.

2. Many of us like sandwiches.

3. Sandwiches and chips make a quick lunch.

4. Some of us have to eat lunch on the run.

5. A sandwich is a snap to eat.

6. Sandwiches have many names.

7. You can have a club sandwich.

8. You can have a sub sandwich as well.

9. Take some sandwiches for a picnic lunch.

10. Sit on the blanket and kick back.

Exercise 7 · Find It: Short Vowels

▶ Read the text below.

▶ Highlight words with short vowels.

▶ Sort the highlighted vowels according to their vowel sound.

▶ Write the words in the correct column.

> **from "What's for Lunch?"**
>
> Most of us take time for lunch. What do you like to eat? Many of us like sandwiches. Sandwiches and chips make a quick lunch. Some lunch times are not very long. Some of us have to eat lunch on the run. A sandwich is a snap to eat. It's quick and not messy.

ă	ĕ	ĭ	ŏ	ŭ

Unit 12 · Lesson 1

Exercise 8 · Masterpiece Sentences

▸ Select nouns from Exercise 5 as the subjects of your **Masterpiece Sentences**.

▸ Select one noun from each category: people, places, things, and ideas.

▸ Write a base sentence and then expand your sentence.

people	

Who (what) did it?	What did they (he, she, it) do?

Base sentence:

_____

Expand your sentence:

_____

places	

Who (what) did it?	What did they (he, she, it) do?

Base sentence:

_____

Expand your sentence:

_____

(continued)

things

Who (what) did it?	What did they (he, she, it) do?

Base sentence:

_____

Expand your sentence:

_____

ideas

Who (what) did it?	What did they (he, she, it) do?

Base sentence:

_____

Expand your sentence:

_____

Exercise 1 · Say and Write

▶ Write the letter or letters for each sound your teacher says.

▶ Say the sound as you write the letters.

▶ Add the correct diacritical mark over the vowel letter to signal the short vowel sound.

1. _____   2. _____   3. _____   4. _____   5. _____

6. _____   7. _____   8. _____   9. _____   10. _____

Exercise 2 · Listening for Sounds in Words

▶ Put an X where you hear / ch / in the words your teacher says.

1. ▢▢▢   6. ▢▢▢

2. ▢▢▢   7. ▢▢

3. ▢▢▢   8. ▢▢

4. ▢▢▢   9. ▢▢

5. ▢▢▢   10. ▢▢▢▢

Exercise 3 · Count It

▶ Read each word.

▶ Fill in the chart with the number of letters and sounds in each word.

	How many letters are in the word?	How many sounds are in the word?
1. size		
2. longed		
3. picnic		
4. exam		
5. stretched		
6. billed		
7. branch		
8. express		
9. bake		
10. thrust		

Exercise 4 · Fill In: Suffixes and Tenses

▸ Fill in the blanks below with words from the **Answer Box**. (One word is not used.)

Answer Box

was	past
am	present progressive
are	past progressive
will	suffix
is	third
were	future
present	tense

1. Some verbs have **-ed** as a _____ to signal _____ tense.

2. The verbs that have **-s** or **-es** as a suffix are _____ person singular, _____ tense verbs.

3. We use the helping verbs _____, _____, or _____ and the **-ing** form to make the _____ _____.

4. We use the helping verb _____ to make the _____ tense.

5. We use the helping verbs _____ or _____ and the **-ing** form to make the _____.

Exercise 5 · Rewrite It: Verb Tenses

▶ Read the present tense sentence in the first column and underline the verb.

▶ Change the verb to the new tense listed in the middle column.

▶ Remember to delete any suffix first.

▶ Remember to use the **Doubling Rule** when needed.

Sentence in Present Tense	New Tense	New Sentence
Example: I <u>munch</u> the crisp drumstick.	Past tense	I _____munched_____ the crisp drumstick.
Example: Rosa <u>catches</u> the bus.	Future tense	Rosa _____will catch_____ the bus.
Example: The gull <u>pecks</u> the clamshell.	Past progressive	The gull _____was pecking_____ the clamshell.
1. Chad flips chicken on the grill.	Past tense	Chad _____ chicken on the grill.
2. Clem mixes mud and twigs to make bricks.	Future tense	Clem _____ mud and twigs to make bricks.
3. Scott ships shellfish to shops in Sweden.	Present progressive	Scott _____ shellfish to shops in Sweden.
4. Lin blocks Beth's strong shot.	Past tense	Lin _____ Beth's strong shot.
5. Frank digs clams from the sand and mud.	Past progressive	Frank _____ clams from the sand and mud.
6. Beth and Lin switch sides at half time.	Future tense	Beth and Lin _____ sides at half time.
7. A huge fish flops on the deck.	Past tense	A huge fish _____ on the deck.

(continued)

Exercise 5 (continued) · Rewrite It: Verb Tenses

Sentence in Present Tense	New Tense	New Sentence
8. Insects buzzed around the plants.	Present progressive	Insects _____ around the plants.
9. The tall man fetches sticks for his dog.	Future tense	The tall man _____ sticks for his dog.
10. Sal's pet chipmunk Rocky jumps on Sal's lap when Sal claps his hands.	Past tense	Sal's pet chipmunk Rocky _____ on Sal's lap when Sal _____ his hands.

Exercise 6 · Identify It: Noun Functions

▸ Read each sentence.

▸ Decide on the function of the underlined noun. Is it the:

  1. Subject

  2. Direct Object

  3. Object of a Preposition

▸ Fill in the bubble to mark the answer.

▸ Check and revise your answers with your teacher.

	Subject	Direct Object	Object of a Preposition
1. My sister won the tennis <u>match</u>.	○	●	○
2. We'll go after the <u>picnic</u>.	○	○	●
3. The <u>sandwich</u> wasn't hot.	○	○	○
4. The plant makes many <u>products</u>.	○	○	○
5. The <u>cakes</u> in that bakery are fantastic.	○	○	○
6. The <u>globe</u> in our classroom is too small.	○	○	○
7. He sold men's hats in his <u>shop</u>.	○	○	○
8. She bought a <u>scale</u>.	○	○	○
9. We got a ticket on the <u>express</u>.	○	○	○
10. I forgot the <u>joke</u>.	○	○	○

Exercise 1 · Listening for Sounds in Words

▸ Listen to each word your teacher says.

▸ Identify the position of the blend or digraph in the word.

▸ Write the letters for the blend or digraph in the box to show the position.

▸ Circle the digraphs.

1.

2.

3.

4.

5.

6.

7.

8.

9.

10.

Exercise 2 · Listening for Word Parts

▸ Listen to each word.

▸ Write the part that your teacher repeats.

▸ Choose *five* words to practice the **Doubling Rule** using the **Double It** template.

1. _____   2. _____   3. _____   4. _____   5. _____

6. _____   7. _____   8. _____   9. _____   10. _____

Exercise 3 · Find It: Essential Words

▸ Find the **Essential Words** for this unit in these sentences.

▸ Underline them. There may be more than one in a sentence.

1. Did you find Dr. Lin?

2. We'll go with Mr. and Mrs. Desoto.

3. Didn't Ms. Cicco tell you?

4. We have only ten minutes to finish.

▸ Write the **Essential Words** in the spaces.

▸ Circle the abbreviations.

_____   _____   _____

_____   _____   _____

Unit 12 · Lesson 3

Exercise 4 · Word Networks: Homophones

▸ Fill in the blanks with the correct homophone.

1. We _____ our fifth game. We are

   number _____ !   (one, won)

2. _____ investors would think that was a   (some, sum)

   huge _____ of money.

3. If they _____ animals on the ship, they   (find, fined)

   will be _____ .

4. Kids have _____ this test in the _____.   (passed, past)

5. They're over _____ in _____ red truck.   (their, there)

Exercise 5 · Verb Tense Review

▸ Read each base verb in the middle column.

▸ Write the past and future tense forms of the verbs in the chart below.

▸ The first one is done as an example.

	Past	Base Verb	Future
1.	added	add	will add
2.		bake	
3.		bank	
4.		block	
5.		bug	
6.		fade	
7.		fish	
8.		hope	
9.		hunt	
10.		invest	
11.		live	
12.		pitch	
13.		pull	
14.		stretch	
15.		tape	

Unit 12 · Lesson 3

Exercise 6 · Identify It: Irregular Past Tense Verbs

▸ Preview the irregular past tense verbs on the chart in the *Student Text,* page 182.

▸ Read the four sentences below.

▸ In each sentence, circle the irregular past tense verb.

▸ On the line at the right, write the base form of the verb.

▸ Check your answers with your teacher.

1. He forgot his lunch ticket. _____

2. They lent it to her sister. _____

3. She thrust the ball into the basket. _____

4. The plant withstood the heat. _____

5. They went to the game. _____

Exercise 7 · Use the Clues

▸ Use word substitution clues to define **muffuletta.**

▸ Circle the vocabulary word and read the text surrounding it.

▸ Circle the words that are a substitute for the new word.

▸ Underline details that provide more explanation.

---

from "Making Hero Sandwiches"

People from southern Italy introduced this kind of sandwich. It was filled with salami, cheese, peppers, olives, and oil. What was the grandfather of the sub? It was probably the muffuletta. People in New Orleans still love this traditional sandwich. Round Sicilian bread is toasted. It is filled with fresh salami, cheese, olive salad, and olive oil. After World War II, Italian food became popular around the world.

▸ Write a definition based on the circled and underlined clues.

▸ Verify your definition with the dictionary or www.yourdictionary.com.

muffuletta–_____

_____

_____

Exercise 8 · Answer It

▶ Underline the signal word.

▶ Answer in complete sentences.

1. After reading this article, explain what ingredients you would use to make a hero sandwich.

_____

_____

_____

_____

_____

(continued)

Exercise 8 (continued) · Answer It

2. Draw a Venn diagram to compare and contrast the ingredients of a hero sandwich made by someone in Italy with those of a hero sandwich made by someone in New Orleans.

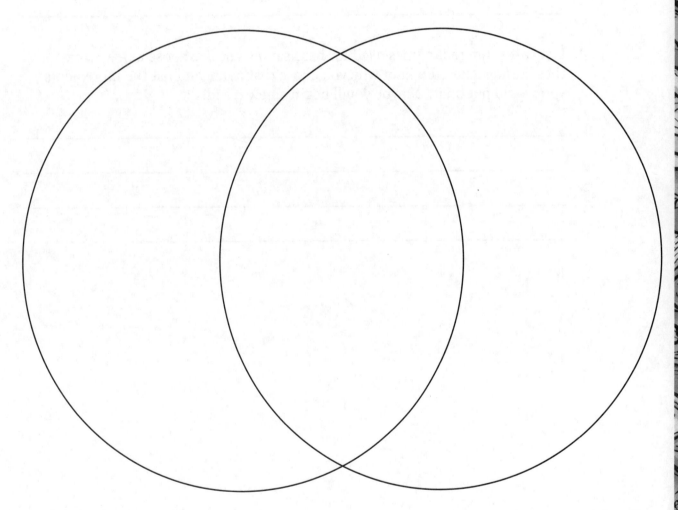

(continued)

Exercise 8 *(continued)* · **Answer It**

3. Describe how the *sub* sandwich got its name.

_____

_____

_____

_____

4. List three different names used for hero sandwiches. Choose a new name for these sandwiches. Explain why you chose that name and list the ingredients you would put on it. Maybe you'll begin a new trend!

_____

_____

_____

_____

Exercise 1 · Listening for Sounds in Words

▸ Put an X where you hear the phoneme your teacher says.

1.
2.
3.
4.
5.
6.
7.
8.
9.
10.

Unit 12 · Lesson 4

Exercise 2 · Fill In: Noun Suffixes

▸ Fill in the blanks below with words from the **Answer Box.**

▸ Some words will be used more than once.

Answer Box

singular
suffix
possessive
plural

1. Most nouns add **-s** as a _____ to show that they are

   _____ .

2. The noun suffix **-'s** shows that the noun is _____

   and _____ .

3. The noun suffixes **-es'** or **-s'** show that a noun is

   _____ and _____ .

4. A noun without a _____ is usually a singular noun.

5. In the sentence, *The egg's shell broke when it fell*, the word **egg's** is

   _____ .

Exercise 3 · Rewrite It: Noun Suffixes

▸ Rewrite each singular noun into the other forms.

Singular Noun	Singular Possessive Noun	Plural Noun	Plural Possessive Noun
1. bank			
2. home			
3. ranch			
4. crop			
5. sandwich			
6. wing			
7. branch			
8. month			

Unit 12 · Lesson 4

Exercise 4 · More Rewrite It: Noun Suffixes

▸ Read the first sentence.

▸ Rewrite the sentence so that the underlined singular noun in the first column is plural in the second column.

▸ Reread the sentence with the plural noun to check your work.

Singular Noun Underlined	Change to Plural Form
They cut the <u>crust</u> off the sandwich. The <u>clam's</u> shell cracked on the rock.	They cut the __crusts__ off the sandwich. The __clams'__ shells cracked on the rock.
1. His father rushed to the shop to get the cake <u>mix</u>.	1. His father rushed to the shop to get the cake _____ .
2. They had to bake a <u>cake</u> for the picnic.	2. They had to bake _____ for the picnic.
3. Lisa helped her father frost the <u>boss's</u> cake.	3. Lisa helped her father frost the _____ cake.
4. They packed the cakes into the <u>basket</u> and put them in the van.	4. They packed the cakes into the _____ and put them in the van.
5. The <u>boss</u> wanted to eat up all the <u>cake</u>.	5. The _____ wanted to eat up all the _____ .

Exercise 5 · Tense Timeline

▸ Listen to each sentence your teacher reads.

▸ Identify and write the verb or verb phrase under the correct position in each chart.

▸ Expand the verb to include five additional forms on the **Tense Timeline**. Use the model your teacher has created on the overhead transparency.

1. I **hope** to find a space to rent.

Past	Present	Future

2. We **pulled** the drapes about five o'clock.

Past	Present	Future

3. He **will forget** something.

Past	Present	Future

4. We **are investing** everything in stocks.

Past	Present	Future

(continued)

Unit 12 · Lesson 4

5. She **will be stretching** the fabric.

Past	Present	Future

Exercise 6 · Blueprint for Reading: Time Sequence Transition Words

▶ Highlight the main ideas in blue.

▶ Put a circle around the transition words: **First, Second, Next, Then, After that,** and **Finally**.

---

from "Making Hero Sandwiches"

First, hold a loaf of French bread on its side. Second, slice the bread in half lengthwise. Next, layer on slices of meat and cheese. Ham and salami can be used. Provolone, Swiss, or American cheese can be used. Then, top with lettuce and tomato. After that, add onions, pickles, olives, and hot peppers. Hot peppers and onions are optional. Finally, spread on mayonnaise or mustard. Other condiments can be added, too. A drizzle of Italian salad dressing adds a little spice. At last, be a hero. Eat that sandwich!

Exercise 7 · Blueprint for Writing: Outline (Book B)

1. _____
    ▸ _____
    ▸ _____

2. _____
    ▸ _____
    ▸ _____

3. _____
    ▸ _____
    ▸ _____

4. _____
    ▸ _____
    ▸ _____

5. _____
    ▸ _____
    ▸ _____

6. _____
    ▸ _____
    ▸ _____

Conclusion _____

Exercise 1 · Say and Write

▸ Listen to each word and designated sound your teacher says.

▸ Write the letters for the vowel sound, blend, or digraph in the designated position.

▸ Add the correct diacritical mark (breve or macron) over the vowel letter.

1. _____   2. _____   3. _____   4. _____   5. _____

6. _____   7. _____   8. _____   9. _____   10. _____

Exercise 2 · Consonant Review

▸ Listen to your teacher read the sentences.

▸ Fill in the blanks.

1. Digraphs are _____ consonants that represent

   _____ sound.

   Give an example: _____

2. Trigraphs are _____ letters that represent

   _____ sound.

   Give an example: _____

3. Blends are _____ consonants that represent

   _____ sounds.

   Give an example: _____

4. Clusters are _____ consonants that represent

   _____ sounds.

   Give an example: _____

Exercise 3 · Sort It: Consonant Combinations

▸ Sort the words with consonant combinations.

▸ Write the word under the correct heading.

▸ Underline the combination in each word.

▸ Some words may fit under more than one column.

▸ Write words that don't fit in any of the first four columns in the column labeled **Other**.

Word Bank

finish	hunt	inches	ship
splash	hope	wings	jump
sprint	close	stretched	tell
catch	stand	thrive	pass

Digraphs	Trigraphs	Blends	Clusters	Other

Exercise 1 · Say and Write

▶ Listen to the word your teacher says.

▶ Write the letter or letters that represent the sound.

▶ Represent the long sound in these words with the vowel letter, an underline, and an **e** (e.g., **a_e**).

1. _____   2. _____   3. _____   4. _____   5. _____

6. _____   7. _____   8. _____   9. _____   10. _____

Exercise 2 · Spelling Pretest 2

▶ Write the words your teacher says.

1. _____   6. _____   11. _____

2. _____   7. _____   12. _____

3. _____   8. _____   13. _____

4. _____   9. _____   14. _____

5. _____   10. _____   15. _____

Exercise 3 · Sort It: Meaning Categories

▸ Read the words in the **Word Bank.**

▸ Sort the words into categories.

▸ Some words may fit in more than one category.

Word Bank

bake	mile	months
sandwich	insects	eggs
scale	ketchup	time
outside	pets	inches
games	clock	chipmunks

Measurement	Cooking	At a Picnic

Exercise 4 · Expand It: Compound Parts

▸ Read each sentence and identify the function of the underlined words.

▸ Fill in the correct bubble to indicate whether each underlined word is the:

    1. S – subject

    2. DO – direct object

    3. OP – object of a preposition

▸ Make the underlined sentence part into a compound and write your new sentence on the line.

▸ Review sentences with your teacher, and make necessary corrections.

1. <u>**Nate**</u> got sandwiches.   S ●   DO ○   OP ○

    Nate and John got sandwiches.

2. <u>**Sandwiches**</u> make a quick lunch.   S ○   DO ○   OP ○

3. I eat sandwiches for <u>**lunch**</u>.   S ○   DO ○   OP ○

4. I like <u>**pickles**</u> on my sandwiches.   S ○   DO ○   OP ○

5. We can get the all the soft drinks into the picnic <u>**basket**</u>.   S ○   DO ○   OP ○

(continued)

Exercise 4 (continued) Expand It: Compound Parts

6. We like **club sandwiches**.   S   DO   OP
                                        ◯   ◯   ◯

_____

7. **Kim** can take the basket to the lake.   S   DO   OP
                                              ◯   ◯   ◯

_____

8. I love **sunshine**.   S   DO   OP
                              ◯   ◯   ◯

_____

9. Nate lent me his passes for the **game**.   S   DO   OP
                                               ◯   ◯   ◯

_____

10. **I** can go to the game after our picnic.   S   DO   OP
                                                 ◯   ◯   ◯

_____

Unit 12 · Lesson 6

Exercise 5 · Use the Clues

▸ Use meaning signals to define **eponym**.

▸ Underline the vocabulary word.

▸ Read text surrounding the unknown word.

▸ Circle the meaning signal.

▸ Underline the words that help define the unknown word.

---

from "Eponymous Sandwiches"

Where do English words get their start? English has hundreds of thousands of words. Some words come from people's names. Others come from places. Sometimes, the name of a person or a place becomes an ordinary, everyday word. We call that word an *eponym*. Years pass. More people start using the word. We use it in conversation. We use it in writing. We forget about the person. We forget about the place. But we keep using words that came from their names!

▸ Write a definition based on the context clues.

▸ Verify your definition with the dictionary or www.yourdictionary.com.

eponym— _____

_____

Exercise 6 · Answer It

▸ Underline the signal word.

▸ Answer in complete sentences.

1. Define eponym in your own words.

_____

_____

_____

_____

2. Explain how sandwich got its name.

_____

_____

_____

_____

3. Identify the way that cheddar, bologna, frankfurter, and hamburger got their names.

_____

_____

_____

_____

4. Explain how your answer to question 3 contrasts from the way sandwiches and pickles got their names.

_____

_____

_____

Exercise 1 · Listening for Sounds in Words

▸ Listen to each word your teacher says.

▸ Identify the vowel sound and decide if it is short or long.

▸ Mark the vowel with the correct diacritical mark to signal the sound.

Short = (˘)
Long = (¯)

1.	a	e	i	o	u	oo
2.	a	e	i	o	u	oo
3.	a	e	i	o	u	oo
4.	a	e	i	o	u	oo
5.	a	e	i	o	u	oo
6.	a	e	i	o	u	oo
7.	a	e	i	o	u	oo
8.	a	e	i	o	u	oo
9.	a	e	i	o	u	oo
10.	a	e	i	o	u	oo
11.	a	e	i	o	u	oo
12.	a	e	i	o	u	oo
13.	a	e	i	o	u	oo
14.	a	e	i	o	u	oo
15.	a	e	i	o	u	oo

Exercise 2 · Rewrite It: Verbs

▶ Read each sentence in the first column and underline the verb.

▶ Rewrite each sentence to fill in the chart with the other verb forms.

Past Tense Sentence	Present Tense	Present Progressive	Future Tense
She <u>shopped</u> a lot.	She shops a lot.	She is shopping a lot.	She will shop a lot.
They tricked Sam.	_____	_____	_____
The dog rushed home.	_____	_____	_____
The clock ticked.	_____	_____	_____
The socks matched.	_____	_____	_____
The big bus stopped.	_____	_____	_____
He waved from the dock.	_____	_____	_____
He tamed the dog.	_____	_____	_____
Dr. Smith called.	_____	_____	_____
We fished from the dock.	_____	_____	_____

Unit 12 · Lesson 7

Exercise 3 · Find It: Verb Forms

▶ Read the first column to identify what verb form to find.

▶ Read each sentence in the second column.

▶ Find and underline the designated verb form.

Can You Find...?	Sentence
Example: Third person singular, present tense verb	He <u>finds</u> a lot of mistakes by checking.
Example: Present tense verb	We often <u>make</u> ham sandwiches for lunch.
Example: Present progressive verb	They <u>are fixing</u> the broken laptop.
Example: Past tense verb	We <u>fixed</u> Sam club sandwiches for the picnic.
Example: Future tense verb	I <u>will wipe</u> the spills from the gas stove.
1. Present tense verb	Each evening we drive up the hill to see the sunset in the west.
2. Present progressive verb	Paul and Bob are running to get back home before lunch.
3. Third person singular, present tense verb	In a big rush, he mixes eggs and ham in a sandwich for his snack.
4. Past tense verb	After our swim, we fished for bass from the dock.
5. Present tense verb	They visit Mrs. White's son at her home.

Exercise 4 · Find It: Noun Suffixes

▸ Read the first column to identify what noun form to find.

▸ Read each sentence in the second column.

▸ Find and underline the designated noun form.

▸ Each sentence contains more than one noun. Be careful to find the right one.

Can You Find...?	Sentence
Example: Singular noun	Because the students worked hard, they did well on the <u>quiz</u>.
Example: Plural noun	All the <u>sandwiches</u> got wet when Bob dropped his backpack into the pond.
Example: Singular possessive noun	<u>Dad's</u> plan is to rest in the shade.
Example: Plural possessive noun	The ranch <u>hands'</u> ropes were in the box next to the shop.
1. Singular noun	The flames shot from the walls of Bill's shack.
2. Singular possessive noun	Bob's snake hissed at the cat and then hid under the desk.
3. Plural possessive noun	They fixed all the ships' masts in the shop by the docks.
4. Singular possessive noun	He lifted his dad's fishing box out of the pond.
5. Plural possessive noun	Who put the candy in the students' desks?

Unit 12 · Lesson 7

Exercise 5 · Combine It: Compound Sentence Parts

▸ Read the sentence pairs below.

▸ From each sentence pair, create a single sentence with one compound part.

▸ On the line, write your new sentence with the compound sentence part.

▸ Review your sentences with your teacher.

1. They have **hot dogs.** They have **sandwiches.**

   _____

2. She made **sub sandwiches.** She made a **cake.**

   _____

3. The Earl of Sandwich liked **games.** The Earl of Sandwich liked **food.**

   _____

4. Dad gave me **a hot sandwich.** Dad gave me **a glass of milk.**

   _____

5. Let's **go outside.** Let's **sit** on a bench.

   _____

Exercise 6 · Draw It: Listening for Information

▸ While listening to **"Eponymous Sandwiches,"** quickly sketch the six different foods and the person or place for which it is named.

Unit 12 · Lesson 7

Exercise 7 · Answer It

▶ Write an answer for the following: Paraphrase how cheddar got its name.

▶ Use replacement words listed with your teacher.

▶ Fill in the blanks to paraphrase how cheddar got its name.

Cheddar got its _____ from the _____ of

Cheddar, where it was _____.

▶ Rewrite the sentence below:

_____

_____

_____

_____

Exercise 1 · Syllable Awareness: Segmentation

▶ Listen to the words your teacher says.

▶ Count the syllables and write the number of syllables in the first column.

▶ Write the letter for each vowel sound you hear.

▶ Add the correct diacritical mark (breve) over the vowel letter to signal the short vowel sounds.

	How many syllables do you hear?	First Vowel Sound	Second Vowel Sound	Third Vowel Sound	Fourth Vowel Sound
1.					
2.					
3.					
4.					
5.					
6.					
7.					
8.					
9.					
10.					

Exercise 2 · Contract It

▸ Combine words to make contractions.

▸ Replace the letters that get squeezed out with an apostrophe (').

▸ Write the contraction.

Read it	Rewrite it
1. he will	
2. did not	
3. she would	
4. are not	
5. they would	
6. we will	
7. I would	
8. it will	
9. does not	
10. were not	

Exercise 3 · Classify It

▸ Use **Unit Vocabulary** in the *Student Text*, page 178, to find words that go together based on meaning.

▸ Fill in the blanks.

1. _____ and _____ are both _____ .

2. _____ and _____ are both _____ .

3. _____ and _____ are both _____ .

4. _____ and _____ are both _____ .

5. _____ and _____ are both _____ .

Exercise 4 · Diagram It: Compound Parts

▶ Read each sentence.

▶ Identify and underline the compound sentence parts in each sentence.

▶ Fill in the diagram for each sentence.

▶ Review your diagrams with your teacher and make corrections.

1. They fix their sandwiches and have lunch.

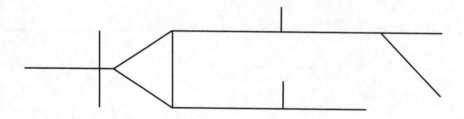

2. We will have lunch and a chat.

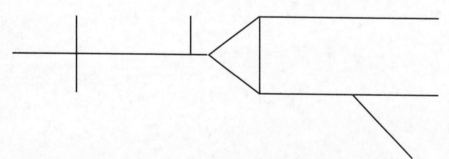

3. The shop makes club sandwiches and hot dogs.

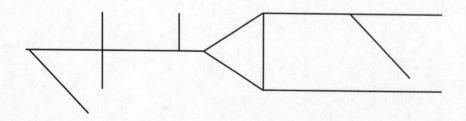

(continued)

4. The Earl of Sandwich liked food and games.

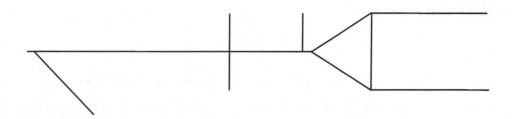

5. Dad got a hot sandwich and a glass of milk.

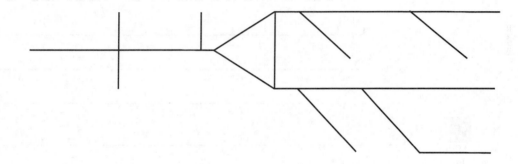

Unit 12 · Lesson 8

Exercise 5 · Blueprint for Writing: Developing Main Ideas

▸ Read each group of details.

▸ Think of a label that tells how the details go together.

▸ Write the label, or main idea, in the box.

Main
Idea

I. _____

   A. _____

   B. _____

   C. _____

   D. _____

Main
Idea

II. _____

   A. _____

   B. _____

   C. _____

   D. _____

Main
Idea

III. _____

   A. _____

   B. _____

   C. _____

▸ Listen to the word your teacher says.

▸ Count the syllables and write the number of syllables in the first column.

▸ Write the letter for each vowel sound you hear.

▸ Add the correct diacritical mark (breve or macron) over the vowel letter to signal a short or long vowel sound.

	How many syllables do you hear?	First Vowel Sound	Second Vowel Sound	Third Vowel Sound
1.				
2.				
3.				
4.				
5.				
6.				
7.				
8.				
9.				
10.				

Exercise 2 · Find It: Nouns

▶ Work with a partner.

▶ Read the selection.

▶ Find and list the kinds of words designated in the chart.

---

from "Eponymous Sandwiches"

Where do English words get their start? English has hundreds of thousands of words. Some words come from people's names. Others come from places. Sometimes, the name of a person or a place becomes an ordinary, everyday word. We call that word an *eponym*. Years pass. More people start using the word. We use it in conversation. We use it in writing. We forget about the person. We forget about the place. But we keep using words that came from their names!

You eat eponymous foods every day. Don't be suspicious. It's true! Many common foods' names come from people or places. The next time you eat a sandwich, think about it. Are you eating eponymous food? Yes! How do you know? The word *sandwich* is an eponym!

(continued)

Exercise 2 (continued) · Find It: Nouns

Singular Nouns or Pronouns	Plural Nouns or Pronouns	Singular Possessive Nouns	Plural Possessive Nouns

Notes

Notes

Notes

Notes

Resources

Resources

ĭ
sit

ă
cat

ŏ
fox

aw
dog

1. _____
2. _____
3. _____
4. _____
5. _____
6. _____
7. _____
8. _____

1. _____
2. _____

1. _____
2. _____
3. _____
4. _____
5. _____
6. _____
7. _____
8. _____
9. _____

1. _____
2. _____

1. _____
2. _____
3. _____
4. _____
5. _____

1. _____
2. _____
3. _____
4. _____
5. _____

1. _____
2. _____
3. _____
4. _____
5. _____

1. _____
2. _____
3. _____
4. _____
5. _____

1. _____
2. _____
3. _____
4. _____
5. _____

1. _____
2. _____
3. _____
4. _____
5. _____
6. _____
7. _____

© Jane Fell Greene.
Based on Moats, L.C. (2003). LETRS: Language Essentials for Teachers of Reading and Spelling, Module 2, (p. 98). Longmont, CO: Sopris West Educational Services. Adapted with permission of the author.

Mouth Position

Type of Consonant Sound	Lips	Lips/Teeth	Tongue Between Teeth	Tongue Behind Teeth	Roof of Mouth	Back of Mouth	Throat
Stops	/ b / / p /			/ t / / d /		/ k / / g /	
Fricatives		/ f / / v /		/ s / / z /			/ h /
Affricatives					/ j /		
Nasals	/ m /			/ n /			
Lateral				/ l /			
Semivowels	/ w /			/ r /	/ y /		

Fluency

Letter-Sound Fluency

	Correct	Errors
1st Try		
2nd Try		

10	qu-	-zz	o	x	i	-ll	-ff	a	-ss	e
20	e	-ck	i	w	e	z	o	y	a	k
30	l	e	n	o	v	i	d	e	g	a
40	a	p	e	j	i	r	o	h	a	e
50	b	o	f	c	a	t	e	s	i	m
60	qu-	-zz	o	x	i	-ll	-ff	a	-ss	e
70	e	-ck	i	w	e	z	o	y	a	k
80	l	e	n	o	v	i	d	e	g	a
90	a	p	e	j	i	r	o	h	a	e
100	b	o	f	c	a	t	e	s	i	m

Letter-Name Fluency

	Correct	Errors
1st Try		
2nd Try		

10	q	z	o	x	i	l	f	a	s	e
20	e	c	i	w	e	z	o	y	a	k
30	l	e	n	o	v	i	d	g	e	a
40	a	p	e	j	i	r	o	h	a	e
50	b	o	f	c	a	t	e	s	i	m
60	q	z	o	x	i	l	f	a	s	e
70	e	c	i	w	e	z	o	y	a	k
80	l	e	n	o	v	i	d	g	e	a
90	a	p	e	j	i	r	o	h	a	e
100	b	o	f	c	a	t	e	s	i	m

Unit 7 — Fluency

Word Fluency 1

	Correct	Errors
1st Try		
2nd Try		

10	set	bell	pest	pet	set	sell	fell	felt	belt	bell
20	fell	pest	felt	pet	sell	felt	pet	pest	fell	belt
30	pet	felt	sell	bell	pest	set	sell	bell	belt	set
40	set	pest	bell	sell	felt	fell	belt	pet	fell	belt
50	felt	bell	fell	pest	sell	felt	set	belt	pet	bell
60	bell	pest	set	pet	set	fell	sell	pet	pest	belt
70	pet	felt	pest	pest	sell	set	fell	belt	sell	felt
80	felt	pet	belt	sell	bell	pest	set	fell	belt	bell
90	pet	set	bell	pest	felt	fell	pet	belt	belt	set
100	bell	pet	fell	sell	felt	felt	belt	pest	bell	sell

Word Fluency 2

	Correct	Errors
1st Try		
2nd Try		

10	bad	bed	will	well	lit	lot	let	bid	bad	bed
20	lot	let	lit	bed	bid	bad	well	will	lot	lit
30	will	well	lit	lot	let	bid	bad	bed	well	will
40	bid	bad	bed	let	lit	lot	bed	bid	bad	let
50	lot	let	lit	bed	bid	bad	let	lit	well	will
60	bed	bad	will	well	lit	lot	well	bid	bad	bed
70	let	bid	bad	bed	let	lit	lot	will	well	bid
80	will	well	lit	lot	let	bid	bad	bed	bid	bad
90	lit	bad	bed	bid	well	will	let	bid	bad	bed
100	will	well	lit	lot	let	bid	bad	bed	well	will

Fluency

Word Fluency 3

	Correct	Errors
1st Try		
2nd Try		

10	text	pest	tell	best	next	neck	speck	spell	tell
20	neck	best	speck	next	speck	tell	best	neck	spell
30	tell	speck	next	best	text	next	pest	spell	text
40	text	best	pest	speck	neck	spell	tell	neck	spell
50	speck	pest	neck	next	speck	text	spell	pest	pest
60	pest	best	text	text	neck	next	tell	best	spell
70	tell	speck	best	next	text	neck	neck	spell	speck
80	speck	tell	spell	pest	best	text	neck	tell	pest
90	tell	text	pest	speck	speck	tell	spell	next	text
100	pest	pest	neck	next	neck	spell	best	pest	next

Word Fluency 4

	Correct	Errors
1st Try		
2nd Try		

10	all	their	into	call	their	our	into	small	call	all
20	into	their	our	into	call	their	small	all	our	small
30	call	our	all	small	their	call	into	our	all	our
40	into	small	their	call	our	small	into	all	our	their
50	all	our	small	their	call	all	our	into	their	small
60	our	all	into	small	all	their	small	our	all	into
70	all	small	our	their	into	our	small	into	their	call
80	into	their	all	small	their	small	our	all	into	our
90	their	small	into	all	small	all	into	their	all	call
100	all	their	our	into	small	all	their	into	call	our

Passage Fluency 1

	Correct	Errors
1st Try		
2nd Try		

Kids log on to the World Wide Web. It is called "the   12
Web." They log on with the Internet. It gives them a   23
path to the Web. They get text from the Web. Kids   34
scan the text. Kids can jot down facts. They get film   45
clips on the Web as well. The Web sends it all to their   58
desktops. The Web spans the planet.   64

Log on. Getting facts is quick. It is a snap. Step on an   77
express track. The Web has facts on all topics. Kids   87
use PCs. PCs help get the facts. Kids use them to   98
draft their text. PCs let kids edit the facts. They print   109
the text. The job ends. Kids do their jobs fast on PCs.   121

A Web site has an address. It has three parts. The   132
first part can be www. This stands for "World Wide   142
Web." It has a dot at the end. The next part gives a   155
name. It has a dot at the end as well. The last part is   169
a group. It does not have a dot at the end.   180

Look at an index on the Web. The list is endless. Get   192
an address. Visit a class. Click. You can get a list of   204
insects. The index has clinics. Click. You can get facts   214
on jogging. "Dot coms" fill the list. Visit the NFL.   224
Click. You can get a list of mascots. Which site will   235
you visit?   237

Look at the past. The Web did not exist. We have   248
it now. It gives facts in a snap. The Web spans the   260
world. The Web sends it all to our desktops.   269

Correct	Errors
1st Try	
2nd Try	

In the past, mail was not fast. There were many 10
steps. Step 1: Get a pen. Step 2: Get a pad of paper. 23
Step 3: Draft text on the pad. Step 4: Get a stamp. 35
Step 5: Drop the letter in the mailbox. The Web lets 46
you skip steps. Sending mail can be quick. Get on the 57
Web. A computer lets you draft text. Next, click on 67
"send." It is sent fast. Expect a prompt reply. 76

Lots of kids log on. IM lets kids visit. Text is sent to 89
pals. They send a fast reply. Kids chat online. There 99
can be many replies. It can get hectic. Kids have a 110
blast with IM. 113

Kids spend lots of time on the Web. In the past, 124
the TV was on a lot. Now, it's on less. Kids are logged 137
on. This is a new trend. How can we tell? A survey 149
was drafted. It asked how kids spend their time. 158
What topped the list? Kids picked the Web. TV lost 168
the top spot. 171

Adults have a job. Ads are sent on the Web. Ads can 183
tempt kids. Kids can be misled. They can be tricked. 193
Adults have to inspect the ads. They can block the 203
bad ads. They look at what is sent. They scan what 214
kids send back. They inspect the sites kids visit. 223
Adults can have a big impact. 229

Letter-Sound Fluency

	Correct	Errors
1st Try		
2nd Try		

10	e	-tch	wh-	o	sh	a	th	i	ch	-ng
20	qu-	-zz	o	x	i	-ll	-ff	a	-ss	e
30	i	-ng	-tch	w	e	ch	o	th	a	-ck
40	v	e	g	o	y	i	w	e	k	a
50	o	-tch	wh-	e	sh	a	th	i	ch	-ng
60	qu-	-zz	o	x	i	-ll	-ff	a	-ss	e
70	i	-ng	-tch	w	e	ch	o	th	k	-ck
80	v	e	g	o	y	i	w	e	a	a
90	o	-tch	wh-	e	sh	a	th	i	ch	-ng
100	qu-	-zz	o	x	i	-ll	-ff	a	-ss	e

Letter-Name Fluency

	Correct	Errors
1st Try		
2nd Try		

10	n	e	o	w	t	h	c	k	g	s
20	e	c	i	w	e	z	o	y	a	k
30	l	n	n	o	v	d	e	g	a	a
40	a	e	e	j	i	r	o	h	h	e
50	b	p	f	c	t	e	s	i	s	m
60	n	e	o	w	t	h	c	k	g	s
70	e	c	i	w	e	z	o	y	a	k
80	l	n	n	o	v	d	e	g	a	a
90	a	e	e	j	i	r	o	h	h	e
100	b	p	f	c	t	e	s	i	s	m

Word Fluency 1

	Correct	Errors
1st Try		
2nd Try		

#									
10	ship	chin	which	thin	chin	chop	shop	ship	witch	wing
20	chin	thin	chop	wing	shop	which	chop	witch	wing	thin
30	which	chop	witch	chin	wing	shop	ship	thin	which	which
40	ship	witch	chin	which	shop	wing	chop	thin	ship	witch
50	which	thin	ship	shop	witch	chin	wing	chop	thin	thin
60	wing	chin	chop	thin	ship	witch	shop	chin	wing	chop
70	witch	ship	chin	wing	chop	thin	which	shop	witch	ship
80	which	wing	witch	shop	chin	ship	chop	thin	which	shop
90	ship	thin	wing	chop	shop	witch	chin	ship	shop	thin
100	which	chop	ship	chin	wing	shop	chin	witch	chop	which

Word Fluency 2

	Correct	Errors
1st Try		
2nd Try		

10	math	thing	patch	math	think	thank	match	thing	path	thick
20	match	think	thick	patch	thick	think	math	thank	patch	path
30	thing	thank	path	think	match	patch	thank	thing	path	math
40	path	think	thick	thing	math	thank	match	math	think	patch
50	match	patch	thick	think	thing	match	thing	path	patch	patch
60	path	thank	match	patch	thick	path	thick	math	thing	thank
70	thing	match	thank	think	thick	patch	think	thing	patch	think
80	path	math	thing	think	thank	match	think	math	patch	math
90	wing	match	math	rank	wing	link	sank	pink	sink	match
100	rank	pink	sank	wing	pink	math	match	link	rank	sink

Word Fluency 3

	Correct	Errors
1st Try		
2nd Try		

10	when	dash	dish	with	wink	than	then	when	link
20	then	than	link	with	with	dish	than	dash	then
30	with	dish	then	when	wink	link	dash	with	dish
40	link	with	dash	then	dish	than	wink	link	dash
50	when	wink	dish	with	than	when	then	then	wink
60	than	dash	link	wink	with	than	dash	dash	than
70	dish	when	dash	then	then	with	with	link	when
80	link	dash	with	than	than	with	when	wink	with
90	when	link	dish	with	dash	than	then	when	wink
100	sing	kings	rings	wing	sing	rings	king	sings	kings

	Correct	Errors
1st Try		
2nd Try		

#							
10	out	write	many	write	word	about	many
20	about	write	any	about	write	word	any
30	out	about	word	any	many	word	any
40	word	many	any	write	many	out	word
50	any	about	many	any	out	write	about
60	write	many	out	about	any	write	word
70	many	any	write	about	write	any	many
80	word	about	word	about	word	write	word
90	any	out	about	word	write	many	write
100	word	about	any	any	many	about	any

Passage Fluency 1

Correct	Errors

1st Try
2nd Try

A ship is moving off the dock. Quick, get on. It is   12
tracking whales. Not to catch them. To catch their   21
songs! Whales sing. It's a fact. Their singing is   30
fantastic! They live in the depths, yet their songs get   40
to the top. They can sing at length. A song can last   52
10 hours! Whales can sing many pitches. The pitch   61
in the song can be shrill. The pitch can be soft. It can   74
blast. Whales can trill in a song. Pitches link and   84
make a song.   87

The whale is the biggest living mammal. It swims   96
past the ship. Inspect it. Its skin is black. It has a   108
gloss to it. It can have a fin on its back. This is not   122
an exotic fish. In fact, it is not a fish at all! It is a   137
mammal. Fish have gills. Whales have lungs.   144

Whales can live in a gam. This is called a pod as well.   157
This is a small group of about 20. They swim as a   169
gam. They sing as a gam. This kinship can help them   180
live. It helps fend off whales that kill.   188

Correct	Errors
1st Try	2nd Try

Woody drifted from job to job. He drilled wells. He   10
picked crops. At 16, he got a guitar as a gift. He did   23
odd jobs. He sang for a living. His songs backtracked   33
to his past. The songs were from his mom and   43
granddad. From them, he crafted a new sound. The   52
past lived on in his songs. His songs were linked with   63
his past. He had to live. For his living, he did many   75
things. His jobs led him across the land.   83

Woody's treks prompted his songs. This vast land   91
impressed him. He was thinking of the grand hills.   100
He was thinking of the land's riches. He wrote "This   110
Land is Your Land." The song expressed his thinking.   119
It was a big hit then. It is still a hit. He wrote many   133
songs. His songs have had an impact.   140

Woody kept writing songs. Then, he got sick. His   149
illness left him helpless. It was sad. Woody is missed.   159
His songs live on. Songs are his lasting gift. We still   170
sing them.   172

Fluency

Letter-Sound Fluency

	Correct	Errors
1st Try		
2nd Try		

10	qu-	-zz	o	x	i	-ll	-ff	a	-ss	u
20	i	-ng	-tch	u	e	ch	o	th	a	-ck
30	v	e	g	o	y	i	w	u	k	a
40	o	-tch	u	e	sh	a	th	i	ch	-ng
50	u	-zz	o	x	i	-ll	-ff	a	-ss	e
60	i	-ng	-tch	u	e	ch	o	th	a	-ck
70	v	e	g	o	y	i	w	u	k	a
80	o	-tch	u	e	sh	a	th	i	ch	-ng
90	qu-	-zz	o	x	i	-ll	-ff	a	-ss	e
100	i	-ng	-tch	u	e	ch	o	th	a	-ck

Letter-Name Fluency

	Correct	Errors
1st Try		
2nd Try		

e	c	i	g	e	z	o	y	a	u	10
n	e	o	w	t	h	c	k	u	s	20
l	u	n	o	v	i	d	e	g	a	30
a	p	e	j	i	r	o	h	a	u	40
b	o	f	c	a	t	e	s	i	m	50
e	c	i	g	e	z	o	y	a	u	60
n	e	o	w	t	h	c	k	u	s	70
l	u	n	o	v	i	d	e	g	a	80
a	p	e	j	i	r	o	h	a	u	90
b	o	f	c	a	t	e	s	i	m	100

Word Fluency 1

	Correct	Errors
1st Try		
2nd Try		

10	much	lunch	such	rush	bunch	lunch	much	munch	brush	crush
20	rush	crush	lunch	much	such	munch	bunch	crush	much	brush
30	lunch	bunch	such	brush	rush	crush	brush	much	lunch	munch
40	bunch	munch	much	crush	lunch	much	lunch	such	rush	rush
50	such	crush	bunch	much	brush	lunch	munch	bunch	brush	such
60	crush	much	brush	such	munch	such	much	rush	lunch	munch
70	brush	lunch	crush	munch	rush	munch	such	lunch	such	lunch
80	lunch	much	brush	rush	such	rush	crush	brush	bunch	such
90	rush	bunch	such	much	bunch	brush	munch	much	crush	brush
100	munch	brush	bunch	lunch	crush	bunch	rush	brush	such	much

Word Fluency 2

	Correct	Errors
1st Try		
2nd Try		

#										
10	bull	bush	full	push	pull	bush	put	full	pulls	puts
20	bush	put	bull	full	bush	pulls	push	pull	puts	push
30	pulls	push	puts	pull	bull	full	bush	put	pull	pulls
40	full	bull	bush	put	pull	bush	pulls	bush	push	puts
50	bush	puts	full	bull	bush	put	push	pulls	pull	put
60	put	push	pulls	put	pull	full	bush	full	bull	puts
70	pull	full	put	pulls	bush	bush	bull	puts	put	push
80	put	pulls	bush	push	put	pull	full	push	puts	bull
90	full	push	push	puts	pull	bull	put	puts	bush	pulls
100	push	full	put	bush	puts	full	pull	bull	pulls	push

Word Fluency 3

	Correct	Errors
1st Try		
2nd Try		

10	from	none	one	some	love	glove	done	front	from	none
20	done	one	glove	love	none	front	one	love	some	from
30	front	love	some	from	one	some	glove	front	done	none
40	one	done	front	none	from	none	some	love	glove	one
50	some	glove	none	done	front	done	glove	one	love	from
60	none	one	love	from	glove	from	none	glove	some	front
70	done	some	glove	one	front	love	from	some	none	glove
80	one	from	front	some	glove	none	done	glove	front	love
90	none	one	love	some	done	glove	love	done	front	one
100	front	none	one	glove	love	done	from	love	some	done

Word Fluency 4

	Correct	Errors
1st Try		
2nd Try		

10	could	should	would	too	two	been	would	been	would	could
20	would	two	should	too	been	too	should	too	should	would
30	could	too	would	been	should	been	two	been	too	should
40	been	should	would	could	two	could	two	would	could	been
50	two	been	could	should	would	should	too	two	should	two
60	should	too	been	would	could	been	should	could	been	should
70	too	could	would	should	been	two	would	been	could	two
80	two	should	been	would	could	been	should	two	would	too
90	could	been	would	should	two	been	would	been	should	two
100	would	two	could	should	been	too	should	would	should	been

Passage Fluency 1

	Errors	
Correct		
1st Try	2nd Try	

What is a bug? Bug is another word for insect. There | 11
are lots of insects. A bug's body has 3 segments. Bugs | 22
have 6 legs. Our bodies do not have 3 segments. Our | 33
bodies do not have 6 legs. Look at some insects. Can | 44
you spot 3 segments? Can you spot 6 legs? | 53
If you can, you have spotted a bug! | 61

Bugs live in—and on—us! Your body has lots of | 72
bugs on it. In fact, some bugs love to live on your | 84
body! You can't spot them. They are too small. Some | 94
bugs love plants, too. Bugs can live on them. Some | 104
bugs love living in beds. Yes, there are bugs that live | 115
in beds! | 117

We fluff the blankets on the bed. Then our eyes get | 128
red. We dust the top of the desk. Then our eyes itch. | 140
What is happening? Bugs are bugging us. It is not | 150
the dust. It's the bugs! To be exact, dust mites are | 161
bugging us. You cannot spot a dust mite with your | 171
eyes. It is too small. Dust mites live on skin cells that | 183
we shed. Some of us get sick from this bug. | 193

Some bugs have wings. Some do not. A bed bug is | 204
a wingless bug. Bed bugs are not big. A bed bug is | 216
much less than an inch long. How much less? Lots. | 226
It is as small as a pencil eraser. It is red. In fact, bed | 240
bugs can be called red bugs. Bed bugs are pests. | 250
They can hatch up to 200 eggs in a flash. That is a lot | 264
of bugs! | 266

The bed bugs live in blankets and mattresses. They | 275
could be living in your bed. Then bed bugs chomp on | 286
us. They suck blood. Gulp! When we rest in bed, they | 297
don't. We get bitten! | 301

Passage Fluency 2

Correct	Errors
1st Try	
2nd Try	

Some bugs live in the grass. One such bug is a chinch | 12
bug. It is a pest. This bug lives in sod. This pest is | 25
bad for grass. Why? When hot months come, chinch | 34
bugs drop eggs in the sod. The eggs hatch. Many of | 45
the small bugs live. These bugs kill grass. How? They | 55
attack grass stems. Then they suck on them. The | 64
grass wilts. This kills the grass. | 70

Bugs live on bushes and crops, too. They can kill | 80
them. How? Bugs chomp on the plants' buds and | 89
stems. When these are missing, plants cannot live. | 97
Bugs can transmit sickness as well. This can kill | 106
plants. Bugs attack crops and kill them. | 113

Bugs transmit sickness to us. They transmit sickness | 121
to pets and plants, too. Getting rid of bugs is a big | 133
job. The task is complex. You have to get to their | 144
nests. They can be anywhere. They are often hidden | 153
from us. | 155

How do you get rid of bugs? You can give them | 166
something toxic. The toxins will kill them. Think | 174
about the impact these toxins have. They kill the bad | 184
bugs. Do they kill helpful bugs as well? What should | 194
we do? | 196

Letter-Sound Fluency

Correct - Errors	1st Try	
	2nd Try	

	10	20	30	40	50	60	70	80	90	100
	o	i	z	o	i	a	z	o	i	a
	u	p	y	u	ch	y	y	u	ch	y
	f	e	u	ll	e	u	u	ll	e	u
	i	j	e	i	th	e	e	i	th	e
	c	r	w	zz	ng	w	w	zz	ng	w
	a	o	v	a	o	sh	v	a	o	sh
	t	h	o	ff	x	o	o	ff	x	o
	e	u	i	e	u	i	i	e	u	i
	s	n	d	ss	qu	tch	d	ss	qu	tch
	m	b	g	ck	a	wh	g	ck	a	wh

Letter-Name Fluency

	Correct	Errors
1st Try		
2nd Try		

10	e	c	i	g	e	z	o	y	a	u
20	l	u	n	o	v	i	d	a	g	e
30	n	e	o	w	t	h	c	k	u	s
40	b	o	f	c	a	t	e	s	i	m
50	a	p	e	j	i	r	o	h	a	u
60	e	c	i	g	e	z	o	y	a	u
70	l	u	n	o	v	i	d	a	g	e
80	n	e	o	w	t	h	c	k	u	s
90	b	o	f	c	a	t	e	s	i	m
100	a	p	e	j	i	r	o	h	a	u

Word Fluency 1

	Correct	Errors
1st Try		
2nd Try		

10	cute	cut	made	mad	hope	hop	pine	pin	fine	fin
20	pin	hope	made	cut	cute	pine	mad	fine	hop	fin
30	hope	mad	pin	made	fin	fine	made	cute	pine	hop
40	cut	pine	hope	fine	pin	mad	hop	made	fin	cute
50	mad	fine	hop	fin	hop	cute	pine	hope	cut	made
60	made	cute	cut	hope	mad	hop	pine	mad	fin	pin
70	hop	cut	cute	made	fin	cute	mad	fin	pin	hope
80	fin	mad	cut	hop	fine	hop	mad	cute	hope	pine
90	mad	fin	fine	pine	hop	pin	cute	hope	cut	made
100	fine	pine	fin	pin	made	cute	hope	hop	mad	cut

Word Fluency 2

	Correct	Errors
1st Try		
2nd Try		

10	five	side	ride	rise	nose	note	take	shape	shade	made
20	shape	ride	note	side	shade	five	rise	made	nose	take
30	rise	note	ride	nose	take	side	shape	five	made	shade
40	ride	shape	take	note	side	rise	made	shade	five	nose
50	take	five	shade	made	ride	shape	note	nose	side	rise
60	note	nose	shape	take	made	five	rise	shade	ride	five
70	ride	take	rise	made	shade	shade	nose	note	five	side
80	shade	made	nose	five	rise	take	ride	side	shape	note
90	nose	rise	made	side	shade	ride	five	take	note	shape
100	made	five	ride	shape	note	shade	nose	rise	take	side

Fluency

Word Fluency 3

	Correct	Errors
1st Try		
2nd Try		

10	use	us	dime	dim	robe	rob	mane	man	quite	quit
20	us	dim	quite	dime	man	quit	use	robe	rob	mane
30	robe	use	dim	mane	rob	dime	quite	quit	man	us
40	dime	man	quit	use	robe	robe	mane	dim	rob	quite
50	quit	quite	man	mane	rob	robe	dim	quite	use	us
60	robe	use	dime	dim	quit	mane	us	rob	rob	man
70	use	dim	rob	us	mane	quite	robe	man	quit	dime
80	us	quite	mane	dime	dim	man	quit	use	rob	robe
90	dime	quit	mane	rob	quite	us	robe	dim	mane	use
100	quite	robe	rob	quit	mane	dime	use	man	us	dim

Word Fluency 4

	Correct	Errors
1st Try		
2nd Try		

Words							#
almost	already	also	although	alone	always	alone	10
already	almost	alone	also	always	almost	although	20
always	alone	also	already	always	alone	almost	30
also	although	alone	always	almost	already	also	40
always	almost	although	alone	also	always	alone	50
almost	already	also	although	always	alone	although	60
alone	almost	always	although	also	already	almost	70
already	also	always	although	also	almost	alone	80
also	already	always	always	also	alone	although	90
always	almost	although	also	already	almost	always	100

Unit 10 • Fluency   393

Passage Fluency 1

	Correct	Errors
1st Try		
2nd Try		

Time is passing. How can we tell? The sun shines on | 11
us. Our planet moves. Time passes. We track time | 20
as our planet moves. This is the basis for time. Think | 31
of the past. People made things to track time. They | 41
stuck a stick in the sand. The stick's shade moved. It | 52
moved as our planet did. Our planet spun in space. | 62
The shade moved. Time passed. The shade shifted. | 70

Next, came sundials. Sundials tracked the sun's | 77
shade. How? An object with three sides sat on the | 87
sundial. It cast the shade in an exact spot. It let | 98
people guess the time. That was fine if the sun was | 109
out. What if it was not? They made candles. They | 119
made notches in the wax. At sunset, people lit them. | 129
They lit them at the top. They noted the time passing. | 140
The wax melted as time passed. The flame made the | 150
wax melt. They watched the candles. They could | 158
guess the time for sunrise. | 163

An hourglass was not like these things. It had sand | 173
inside. The sand inside tracked passing time. Sand | 181
moved from the top. It went into a hole. It dropped | 192
into the base. Was this time exact? It was not. A long | 204
time passed. Then exact clocks came. We take clocks | 213
for granted. What was life like without clocks? | 221

Where do you live? What time zone is it? The | 10
globe has 24 time zones. They are about the same | 20
size. Time zone lines run from pole to pole. The | 30
continental U.S. has four time zones. You cross from | 39
zone to zone. You must adjust the clock. Set the time | 50
ahead or back an hour. Take a ride. Drive west in the | 62
U.S. You drive into the next time zone. Set your clock | 73
back one hour. You have an extra hour. Drive east. | 83
You cross into another time zone. This time you lose | 93
an hour. Adjust your clock. | 98

Think about planes. Planes can cross many time | 106
zones. A plane takes off from Wisconsin. It is | 115
6:00 p.m. It crosses 12 time zones. The plane lands. | 125
It is 6:00 a.m.! On that side of the globe, it is the next | 139
day! It was a long trip. Your body's clock tells you one | 151
time. Check the time in this zone. The times don't | 161
match! The clock inside your body is mixed up. You | 171
have jet lag! Rest helps. It takes time to adjust. | 181

What time is it? We have 12-hour clocks in our | 191
homes. It is 5:00. Is it 5:00 a.m.? Is it 5:00 p.m.? Use a | 205
24-hour clock. It can help. With it, 5:00 p.m. is 1700 | 216
hours. 5:00 a.m. is 0500 hours. Can you tell time like | 227
this? Telling time is quite a skill! | 234

Letter-Sound Fluency

	Correct	Errors
1st Try		
2nd Try		

10	o	u	ll	i	zz	a	ff	e	ss	ck
20	i	ch	e	th	ng	o	x	u	qu	a
30	a	y	u	e	w	sh	o	i	tch	wh
40	o	u	ll	i	zz	a	ff	e	ss	ck
50	i	ch	e	th	ng	o	x	u	qu	a
60	a	y	u	e	w	sh	o	i	tch	wh
70	o	u	ll	i	zz	a	ff	e	ss	ck
80	i	ch	e	th	ng	o	x	u	qu	a
90	a	y	u	e	w	sh	o	i	tch	wh
100	o	u	ll	i	zz	a	ff	e	ss	ck

Letter-Name Fluency

	Correct	Errors
1st Try		
2nd Try		

10	l	u	o	v	i	d	a	g	e
20	n	e	w	t	h	c	k	u	s
30	b	o	f	c	t	e	s	i	m
40	a	p	j	i	r	o	h	u	a
50	e	c	g	e	o	z	y	a	u
60	l	u	o	v	i	d	a	g	e
70	n	e	w	t	h	c	k	u	s
80	b	o	f	c	t	e	s	i	m
90	a	p	j	i	r	o	h	u	a
100	e	c	g	e	o	z	y	a	u

Word Fluency 1

	Correct	Errors
1st Try		
2nd Try		

frame	flame	plate	grape	plane	track	trick	clock	block	black	10
black	block	clock	frame	flame	plate	grape	plane	track	trick	20
black	block	frame	flame	plate	grape	plane	track	trick	clock	30
plane	track	grape	plane	track	black	block	frame	flame	plate	40
flame	frame	black	plane	grape	track	trick	clock	plate	trick	50
frame	flame	plate	grape	black	plate	track	trick	clock	grape	60
plane	track	grape	block	plane	grape	black	plate	frame	plane	70
black	block	frame	flame	frame	black	plane	track	grape	block	80
block	frame	flame	plate	grape	plane	track	trick	clock	block	90
black	block	frame	black	block	frame	block	flame	plate	grape	100

Correct	Errors
1st Try	
2nd Try	

10	scrap	strap	spoke	string	skill	string	swing	skill	still	spill
20	string	swing	skill	scrap	spoke	scrap	strap	spoke	stone	stock
30	scrap	strap	skill	spill	stock	spoke	stone	stock	string	swing
40	stock	string	swing	scrap	strap	spill	scrap	strap	spoke	stone
50	scrap	strap	spoke	stone	skill	string	swing	skill	still	spill
60	scrap	strap	skill	spill	stock	spoke	stone	stock	string	swing
70	spill	scrap	strap	spoke	stone	skill	swing	skill	spoke	stone
80	stock	string	swing	scrap	strap	swing	strap	scrap	spoke	scrap
90	strap	spoke	stone	stock	string	stock	string	swing	still	spill
100	string	swing	skill	scrap	spoke	scrap	strap	spoke	stone	stock

Word Fluency 3

	Correct	Errors
1st Try		
2nd Try		

10	grasp	crust	rest	clasp	grasp	dump	dusk	dent	dust	spend
20	dump	dusk	dent	spend	grasp	grasp	crust	rest	chest	dust
30	crust	rest	clasp	chest	crust	grasp	dent	spend	grasp	dusk
40	spend	dust	grasp	rest	spend	dump	chest	grasp	crust	dent
50	grasp	crust	rest	clasp	grasp	crust	dusk	dump	dust	chest
60	clasp	grasp	dust	dent	spend	crust	dent	crust	spend	dust
70	dump	dent	rest	chest	dusk	rest	grasp	dusk	rest	chest
80	crust	clasp	grasp	rest	grasp	spend	spend	grasp	dump	grasp
90	spend	spend	dusk	dent	crust	dust	grasp	dump	spend	dent
100	grasp	dust	dent	crust	dusk	crust	dust	rest	grasp	dust

	Correct	Errors
1st Try		
2nd Try		

each	every	very	body	know	thought	each	body	every	very	10
every	body	each	know	thought	very	body	thought	know	each	20
know	each	thought	very	body	every	very	every	body	thought	30
very	body	know	each	every	thought	know	each	thought	very	40
thought	very	every	body	know	each	body	thought	each	every	50
body	thought	know	every	each	each	thought	very	know	body	60
each	every	thought	body	know	very	each	thought	each	very	70
very	body	each	know	every	thought	very	each	every	each	80
every	very	body	know	thought	body	very	very	very	thought	90
know	very	body	each	thought	every	thought	each	body	every	100

Passage Fluency 1

	Errors	
Correct		
1st Try	2nd Try	

What can fly without wings? What has a tail but   10
not a face? What gets stuck on a branch in the   21
comics? What can you pull but not push? You got it.   32
It's a kite.   35

Think about a fine, strong wind. In one hand is a   46
stick. On the stick is lots of string. In the left hand is   59
a kite. The string is tied to the kite's frame. Undo the   71
string as you run. The wind lifts the kite into the air.   83
The string slips from your hand. If there's wind, the   93
kite is up. It's off! It takes skill. It takes wind. It takes   106
luck! The kite drifts up until it is just a speck.   117

Where did kites come from? What prompted the   125
thought? It was the wind. The wind grabbed a man's   135
hat. It was still tied to his chin. He felt the strong   147
wind's tug. It made him think. What if I tied fabric   158
to a string? What if I held the string in my hand? The   171
wind would make the cloth fly. He made it. From this   182
thought, kites came about.   186

When was this? It was 200 BC! At this time, kites   197
were not for fun. Kites were used to pass thoughts.   207
They helped make contact. In combat, kites sent   215
coded facts. The facts could help one side win. Kites   225
were used like this for a long time.   233

Correct	Errors
1st Try	
2nd Try	

Kites can have long tails. Without a tail, the diamond   10
kite spins. The tail adds mass. It stops the spinning.   20
Some kites can fly without tails. The box kite is one.   31
Its shape lets it fly and not spin. The shape of a kite   44
and its use are linked.   49

Kites have been used in combat. We know they sent   59
coded facts. In fact, kites have had many uses. They   69
have helped us grasp things about our planet. How   78
hot is it up in the sky? In the past, kites helped us   91
know. One string held many kites. A strong wind   100
lifted them up. When all of the kites landed, they   110
had the facts.   113

We know who Ben Franklin is. Did you know the   123
story about how he used kites? Franklin gazed at   132
lightning in the sky. He asked himself, "What sets   141
it off? Can I catch it? Can I use it?" Big flashes lit   154
up the sky. Ben sent up a kite. A key hung from the   167
string. The lightning hit the key. This gave him ideas.   177
In time, someone would expand on what he did.   186

Big things have come from small kites. They were   195
used in combat. They helped us know about our   204
planet. They prompted us to invent things. We still   213
use kites. We use them when the wind is strong. Get   224
a kite. Have fun!   228

Letter-Sound Fluency

	Correct	Errors
1st Try		
2nd Try		

10	o	u	ll	i	zz	a	ff	e	ss	ck
20	i	ch	e	th	ng	o	x	u	qu	a
30	a	y	u	e	w	sh	o	i	tch	wh
40	o	u	f	i	c	a	t	e	s	m
50	i	p	e	j	r	o	h	u	n	b
60	z	y	u	e	w	v	o	i	d	g
70	o	u	ll	i	zz	a	ff	e	ss	ck
80	i	ch	e	th	ng	o	x	u	qu	a
90	a	y	u	e	w	sh	o	i	tch	wh
100	z	y	u	e	w	v	o	i	d	g

Letter-Name Fluency

	Correct	Errors
1st Try		
2nd Try		

10	n	e	o	w	t	h	c	u	k	s
20	b	o	f	c	a	e	s	i	m	a
30	a	p	e	j	r	o	h	u	a
40	e	c	i	g	o	z	d	y	a	u
50	l	u	n	v	i	d	a	g	e
60	n	e	o	w	t	h	c	u	k	s
70	b	o	f	c	a	e	s	i	m	a
80	a	p	e	j	r	o	h	u	a
90	e	c	i	g	o	z	d	y	a	u
100	l	u	n	v	o	a	g	e

Word Fluency 1

	Correct	Errors
1st Try		
2nd Try		

10	five	late	live	state	hate	side	ride	grade	fade	dive
20	state	hate	side	five	ride	live	late	fade	dive	grade
30	side	dive	live	state	five	fade	grade	hate	ride	late
40	live	side	late	fade	grade	dive	state	five	hate	ride
50	five	fade	hate	live	side	ride	grade	dive	late	state
60	ride	late	fade	dive	grade	state	five	hate	side	live
70	grade	five	ride	state	hate	live	side	fade	late	hate
80	late	dive	grade	hate	five	ride	fade	five	live	state
90	hate	live	dive	ride	late	grade	side	state	fade	five
100	fade	late	side	state	five	dive	ride	hate	live	grade

	Correct	Errors
1st Try		
2nd Try		

catch	match	side	much	ranch	branch	branches	thin	think	thing	10
ketchup	five	catch	thin	crutch	think	munch	thing	side	crust	20
munch	thin	ketchup	five	catch	thing	side	crust	think	crutch	30
thin	munch	think	catch	crust	ketchup	thing	crutch	five	side	40
think	crutch	crust	munch	side	catch	crust	ketchup	thin	five	50
thin	think	crutch	five	ketchup	munch	catch	side	thing	thing	60
crust	thing	five	thin	crutch	side	catch	munch	catch	ketchup	70
crutch	thin	crust	side	think	five	munch	thing	think	catch	80
five	side	think	crutch	crust	thin	ketchup	catch	thing	munch	90
side	catch	thing	munch	ketchup	munch	crust	five	thin	think	100

Word Fluency 3

	Correct	Errors
1st Try		
2nd Try		

passed	past	jump	with	within	withstand	passing	wing	jumping	jumped	10
jump	passing	passed	junk	shade	jumping	paste	shaking	shaking	shake	20
pasted	passed	jumping	jump	passed	shaking	shake	passing	shade	junk	30
shake	junk	jump	passed	shade	paste	jumping	jump	shaking	40	
shade	pasted	jumping	shake	passed	passing	junk	shaking	paste	50	
jumping	shade	passing	junk	shaking	jump	passed	shake	shake	60	
passed	passing	jumping	jump	shaking	shade	pasted	junk	paste	70	
jump	jumping	paste	shake	junk	passed	shade	shade	shaking	80	
junk	jump	shake	jumping	shade	pasted	passing	shaking	paste	passed	90
passing	paste	pasted	junk	jump	shaking	passed	shake	shade	jumping	100

Word Fluency 4

	Correct	Errors
1st Try		
2nd Try		

Dr.	Mr.	Mrs.	Ms.	find	only	Dr.	Ms.	Mr.	Mrs.	10
Mr.	Ms.	Dr.	find	only	Mrs.	Ms.	only	find	Dr.	20
find	Dr.	only	Mrs.	Ms.	Mr.	Mrs.	Mr.	Ms.	only	30
Mrs.	Mrs.	find	Dr.	Mr.	only	find	Dr.	only	Mrs.	40
only	only	Mr.	Ms.	find	Dr.	Ms.	only	Dr.	Mr.	50
Ms.	Ms.	find	Mr.	Dr.	Mrs.	only	Mrs.	find	Ms.	60
Dr.	Mr.	only	Mrs.	Ms.	find	Dr.	Mr.	only	Mrs.	70
Mrs.	find	Dr.	find	Mr.	only	Mrs.	Ms.	Mr.	Dr.	80
Mr.	only	Mrs.	Ms.	only	Dr.	Mr.	find	Mrs.	only	90
find	Dr.	Ms.	Dr.	Mr.	only	find	Dr.	Ms.	Mr.	100

		Errors
	Correct	
1st Try		
2nd Try		

How did the sandwich get its name? It came from | 10
a man. His name was Sandwich. He invented it! | 19
Sandwich loved games. In the games, he used his | 28
hands. His hands could not be messy. Thinking of | 37
this, he made a sandwich. It was quick to eat. It kept | 49
his hands from getting messy. It fit the bill! He could | 60
use one hand to eat. This left one hand for the game. | 72

Ask for a sandwich. What name did you use? | 81
Sandwiches have many names. Sandwiches come | 87
in many shapes and sizes. You can have a club | 97
sandwich. You can have a sub sandwich as well. | 106
Do you like ham and swiss on a bun? Make a | 117
sandwich. A club. A sub. Make it thick. Make it thin. | 128
Just put the things you like on it. This makes quite an | 140
inviting sandwich! | 142

Packing a lunch for a picnic? Take some sandwiches. | 151
Pack chips and drinks. Put them in a basket. Bring a | 162
blanket as well. Strap the blanket and the basket to | 172
the back of a bike. Take a long ride to a lake. | 184
You can rest when the trek is finished. Sit on the | 195
blanket and kick back. Then, unpack the basket. It's | 204
time for lunch. | 207

Letter-Sound Fluency Chart

110
100
90
80
70
60
50
40
30
20
10

Correct Letter-Sounds per Minute

Dates:

Unit:

Fluency Charts

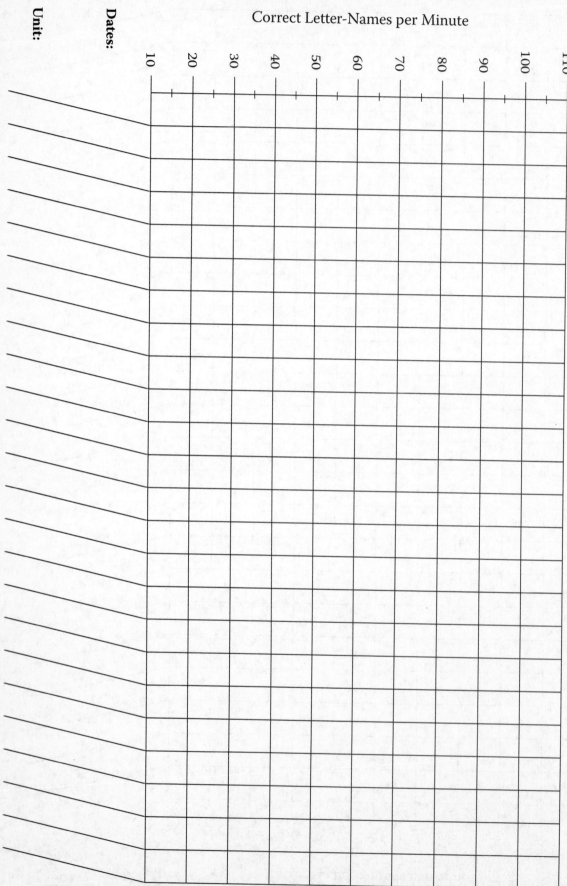

Unit:

Dates:

Correct Letter-Names per Minute

10 20 30 40 50 60 70 80 90 100 110

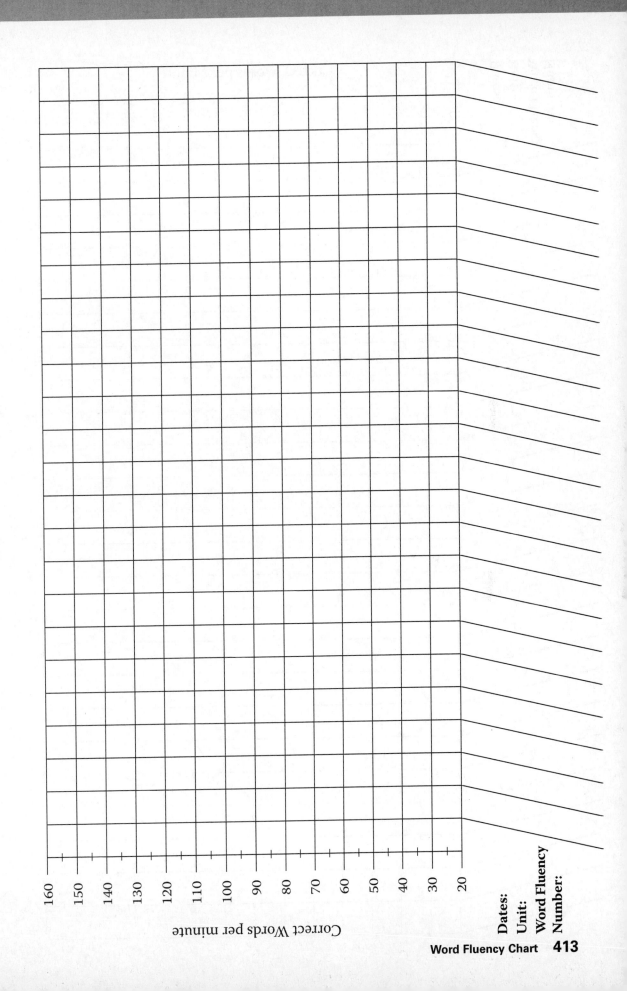

Correct Words per minute

160
150
140
130
120
110
100
90
80
70
60
50
40
30
20

Dates:
Unit:
Word Fluency
Number:

Fluency Charts

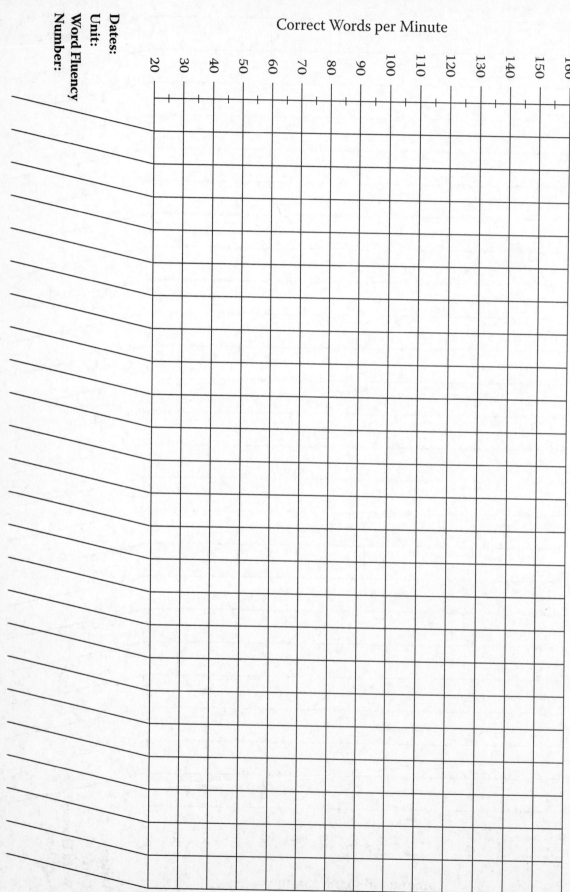

Correct Words per Minute

20 30 40 50 60 70 80 90 100 110 120 130 140 150 160

Dates:
Unit:
Word Fluency
Number:

Correct Words Per _____

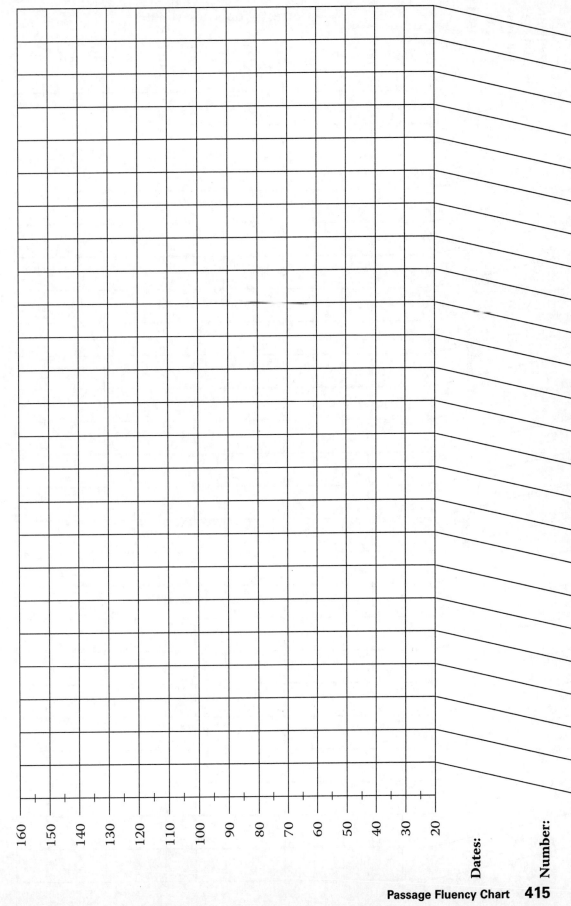

160
150
140
130
120
110
100
90
80
70
60
50
40
30
20

Dates:

Number:

Fluency Charts

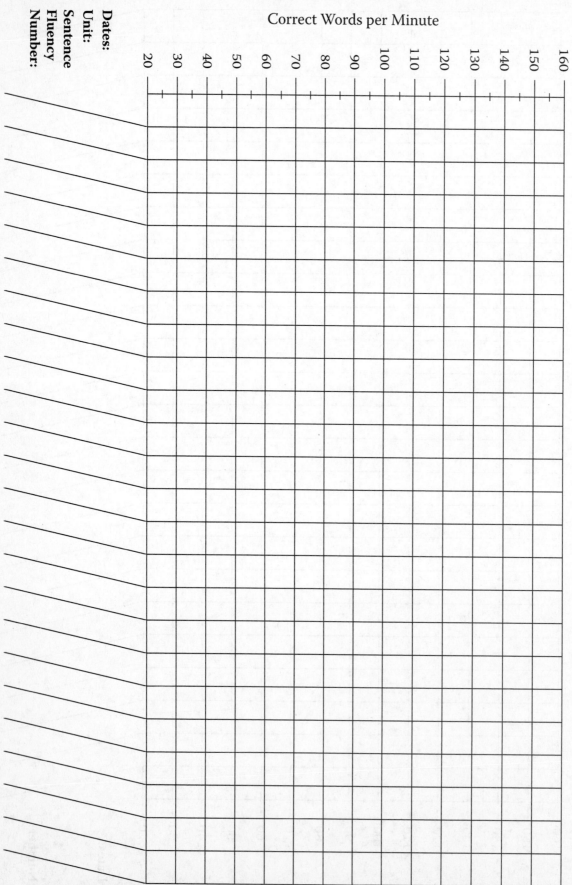

Correct Words per Minute

160 150 140 130 120 110 100 90 80 70 60 50 40 30 20

Dates:
Unit:
Sentence
Fluency
Number:

Essential Word Cards

Unit 7

all	into	small
call	our	their

Unit 8

about	many	word
any	out	write

Unit 9

been	should	two
could	too	would

Unit 10

almost	already	although
alone	also	always

Essential Word Cards

Unit 11

body	every	thought
each	know	very

Unit 12

Dr.	Mrs.	find
Mr.	Ms.	only

Word Building Letter Cards

a	a	b	b	c	c	d
d	f	f	g	g	h	h
i	i	j	j	k	k	l
l	m	m	n	n	o	o
p	p	qu	qu	r	r	s
s	t	t	v	v	w	w
x	x	y	y	z	z	ck
ck	ll	ll	ss	ss	ff	ff
zz	zz					

Word Building Letter Cards

D	C	C	B	B	A	A
H	H	G	G	F	F	D
L	K	K	J	J	I	I
O	O	N	N	M	M	L
S	R	R	Qu	Qu	P	P
W	W	V	V	T	T	S
	Z	Z	Y	Y	X	X

Student _____ Date _____

a _____	c _____	e _____
_____	_____	_____
_____	_____	_____
_____	_____	_____
_____	_____	_____
_____	_____	_____
_____	_____	_____
_____	_____	_____
_____	_____	_____
_____	_____	_____
_____	_____	_____
_____	_____	_____
_____	_____	_____
_____	_____	_____
_____	_____	_____
b _____	d _____	f _____
_____	_____	_____
_____	_____	_____
_____	_____	_____
_____	_____	_____
_____	_____	_____
_____	_____	_____
_____	_____	_____
_____	_____	_____
_____	_____	_____
_____	_____	_____
_____	_____	_____
_____	_____	_____
_____	_____	_____

Bank It

Student _____ Date_____

g	i	k

h	j	l

Bank It

m	o	qu

n	p	r

Bank It

Student _____ Date_____

s	u	x

	v	y

t	w	z